STORIES FROM THE OASIS

Oasis Church

Copyright © 2007 Good Catch Publishing, Beaverton, OR.

All rights reserved. Written permission must be secured from the publisher to use or reproduce any part of this book, except for brief quotations in critical reviews or articles.

This book was written for the express purpose of conveying the love and mercy of Jesus Christ. The statements in this book are substantially true; however, names and minor details have been changed to protect people and situations from accusation or incrimination.

All Scripture quotations, unless otherwise noted, are taken from the New International Version Copyright 1973, 1987, 1984 by International Bible Society.

Published in Beaverton, Oregon, by Good Catch Publishing.
www.goodcatchpublishing.com
V1.1

Printed in the United States of America

Table of Contents

	Acknowledgements	9
	Introduction	13
1	Hungry No More	15
2	Nueva Cada Dia (New Each Day)	55
3	Rebel Boy	77
4	Filled	97
5	The Scar Removed	117
6	Outside Prison Walls	139
	Conclusion	173

Acknowledgements

I would like to thank Barney Huie for the vision he had from the beginning and the effort he put into making this book a reality. This book would not have been published without the amazing efforts of our project manager, Brenna Darazs. Her untiring efforts have pushed this project forward and turned it into a stunning victory. Thank you for your great fortitude and diligence. Thank you also to project manager Jennifer Wade, who oversaw the book's revisions.

I would also like to thank our invaluable proofreader, Melody Davis, for all the focus and energy she has put into perfecting our words. Lastly, I want to extend our gratitude to Evan Earwicker, our graphic artist, whose talent and vision continually astounds us. We are so blessed to have you as a part of this team.

Daren Lindley
President and CEO
Good Catch Publishing

The book you are about to read is a compilation of authentic life stories.
All the facts are true, and all the events are real.
These storytellers have dealt with crisis, tragedy, abuse and neglect and have shared their most private moments, mess-ups and hang-ups in order for others to learn and grow from them.
In order to protect the identities of those involved in their pasts, the names of some storytellers have been withheld or changed.

Introduction

The love, grace and mercy of God are amazing qualities of his nature and character. He accepts us as we are but loves us too much to leave us there. He gently delivers, cares, nurtures and empowers us so we can grow into mighty men and women of God that reflect his saving grace and glory.

We at Oasis Church are proud of those who have courageously revealed to us some of the most painful moments in their lives. In this book, you are going to see firsthand God's love, grace, mercy and redeeming power in action.

These stories offer hope and have not been modified, dramatized, exaggerated or inflated. They are stories of real people who made either less than ideal choices or were victims of insensitive and sometimes savage forces that brought them some of life's greatest difficulties. Their reports are wrenching, yet 100 percent true.

As you witness these true-life experiences, you will be inspired and encouraged to trust God with your pain, your problems and your potential in him.

1
HUNGRY NO MORE
The Story of Christy
Written by Karen Koczwara

"I'm thirsty, Daddy," I whimpered, watching my dad toss the football back and forth with his buddy on the blacktop outside our apartment. His dark hair cascaded around his face, veiling his cold, callous eyes. I scooted to the edge of the porch and sank my head into my hands. Tears welled in my eyes as I licked my dry lips.

"Not now, stupid!" My father briefly glanced over, glaring at me. "Get back upstairs! Now!"

"But, Daddy, I'm so thirsty. I haven't had anything to drink all day," I moaned, the tears now spilling down my cheeks. Their saltiness only added to my parched state.

How can he be so heartless?

"I said, get your a** back upstairs!" My father pounded the football back and forth between his palms. Anger mounted in his voice as he growled at me, his eyes full of disgust. "Can't you see I'm busy?"

But you're always busy, I wanted to cry but didn't dare. He might lunge and strike me. My little 4-year-old body couldn't afford another bruise. I'd have to wear pants all summer long in the dead heat.

"Go long!" my father called out, racing toward his football buddy. He was back in his own little world, obviously done with our conversation.

Stories from the Oasis

I wiped the tears with the back of my hands and wished away the giant hole in my heart. *Just one drink, that's all I ask,* the tiny voice inside cried out. But it wasn't just about the drink. It was about the father who didn't see me, who didn't know me at all.

Out of the corner of my eye, I spotted a small pool of liquid on the blacktop. A pretty rainbow reflected off of it. *Water! Am I really thirsty enough to drink it?* I bounced the idea back and forth in my mind for several moments as my thirst mounted. Beads of sweat pricked my forehead as the sun beat down on me. It might be the only drink I'd get all day.

On impulse, I crawled toward the pool of water and, like a dog at his bowl, stuck my tongue out for a lick. Ugh! It tasted terrible! Out of desperation, I took another lick, and then another. Cringing, I recoiled and realized it wasn't water at all but water mixed with motor oil!

"What the h*** are you doing?" My father dropped his football and charged at me, his eyes slits of rage. "Get your a** upstairs, or I'll beat you!"

No, no, no! Please, Daddy! Don't hurt me again! My legs trembled as I leapt up and ran before he could grab me …

Hungry No More

***

People say home is where the heart is. I wish this could have been true for me growing up. Unfortunately, home was the place I loathed the most. It was where I lived in fear of my father, where I cried myself to sleep and where I wished with all my being that I could run away. My heart was at home, but it was broken, empty, shattered.

When I was 3 years old, my family moved from El Paso, Texas, to California. My mother found work, and my father continued life as a professional raging alcoholic.

His days were spent hitting the bottle and immersing himself in pornography. Food was scarce, and my younger brother and I often went to bed hungry. One particular night, my father turned especially abusive.

"Where's the money?" My father lunged toward my mother the moment she walked through the front door after work.

She sank onto the couch and pulled a wad of cash from her purse. "Here, happy?"

I watched quietly from the kitchen as my father meticulously counted the wad of bills. "This is it?" he barked.

"You know how much I make. Don't give me a

Stories from the Oasis

bad time. At least I ..." my mother started to argue, then bit her tongue. I knew she didn't want to anger him anymore.

Hand the money over, and no one gets hurt.

"Go to the store, and get me some food! Now!" My father thrust a $20 bill at my mother. "You know what I like," he added with a sneer.

My mother nodded quietly. "The children, though. They need to ... they haven't eaten ..." Her voice trailed off again.

Say it, Mama! Tell him our cupboards are bare! Tell him our stomachs are growling! Tell him this isn't fair!

But we didn't dare argue with Daddy. No need to add another bruise to the collection. I watched as my mother wearily pulled herself from the couch, grabbed her coat and slunk out the door.

"Stupid b****," my father muttered under his breath, retreating to the kitchen for another beer. He slammed the refrigerator door and turned to glare at me. "What are you lookin' at?" he sneered.

"Sorry," I replied in a small voice, as though I needed to apologize for my existence.

Why is he always so mean?

My mother returned a while later, lugging two large grocery sacks. I watched as she pulled a large package of sausage and biscuits out of the bag and

Hungry No More

fired up the stove.

Please, please let some be for us! I hadn't eaten since last night, and my stomach hurt so badly I wanted to cry.

"Cook it the way I like it!" my father growled, watching from the table where he took long swigs of his beer. "And you better not burn it!"

My mother nodded, her shoulders sagging as she tossed the sausage into the pan. Instantly, a wonderful aroma filled the air. I could practically taste the meat on my lips.

My brother sat beside me, his eyes wide and hopeful. I knew what he was thinking: *Please share it with us!* He, too, hadn't eaten all day. His already tiny frame couldn't afford to shed any more weight.

"Get under the table, you two!" my father growled at us.

We obeyed, hunkering under the kitchen table as the inviting aroma wafted toward us. Something in the pit of my stomach told me we might never see a bite of this wonderful food.

My father took the liberty of piling his plate high with sausage and biscuits. He took one large bite after another, making "mmm" sounds after each bite. "This s*** is good," he announced with a long sigh.

Stories from the Oasis

I wrapped my bony arms around my knees and began to cry.

How can he be so mean? What would it hurt him to share? He didn't earn it, anyway! My poor mother is the one who worked so hard for it!

"Aw, you hungry?" my father drawled with a full mouth. He chomped loudly, driving me to fury. "Here, have a bite." He tossed a piece of biscuit under the table, as though we were two pathetic dogs waiting for scraps.

Shamefully, I grabbed for it, surprised at my own desperation. It tasted so good, warm and buttery. But it was only a tease. I would go to bed hungry tonight — again.

When I was 5, we moved back to Texas to be near our extended family. My father found work at the local bars. It wasn't exactly reputable work, but at least it kept him away from home.

I entered the first grade, and my brother began kindergarten. The few hours spent at school were a welcome relief from the horrors of my home. My father continued to serve as our primary caregiver, if that title could even suffice. We were late for school every morning as our nights were spent hanging out at the local bars where he worked. At the young age of 7, I had seen more filth than most people have in a lifetime. To me, though, I knew

Hungry No More

no other way. I thought every little girl had a father who drank and worked in a topless bar.

One morning, shortly after I'd arrived at school, I spotted a frantic looking man darting down the halls. He had only one boot on and appeared to be looking for someone. On second glance, I realized it was my father!

"What are you doing here, Daddy?" I cried as he stopped in his tracks.

"Where's your brother?" he hissed, grabbing me tightly by the shoulder.

"In that room," I replied quietly, pointing down the hall. "What's going on?"

"No questions now," he snapped, dragging me down the hall. He yanked open the door to my brother's classroom and stormed in. Moments later, he returned with my brother in tow. "Come on, we gotta get outta here!"

"Daddy, tell me what's going on!" My heart thumped in my chest. Dads weren't supposed to take their kids out of their classrooms without telling the teachers.

Something terrible must have happened! Is it Mama? Oh, please, no!

To my shock, a swarm of cops were waiting outside the school doors. "Put the kids down!" they shouted, guns poised.

Stories from the Oasis

Terrified, I looked up at my father for an explanation. He stopped mid-stride, his eyes darting back and forth as though deciding whether or not to make a run for it.

Is he in trouble? Are the cops going to take him away?

From the schoolyard, a group of kids hollered over the fence. I hung my head, mortified. *How can my father do this to us in front of the whole school? Can't he see what a scene he is causing?*

"Put the kids down!" the cops repeated, closing in on us.

"You can have the girl. I keep the boy," my father conceded.

I glanced over at my brother, my eyes full of terror.

Keep the boy? What will happen to him? No! This isn't right!

"Go to them," my father nudged, pointing at the cops.

Slowly, I stepped forward. The minute I did, my father grabbed my brother, hopped in his beat up El Camino and sped away. My heart sank.

What if I never see my brother again?

"You can trust us," the cops encouraged me, sensing my apprehension. "We're going to take you to a safe place. Your mother will be there."

Hungry No More

I nodded, tears brimming in my eyes. Dozens of children watched in awe from the playground as I gingerly climbed into the cop car. Perhaps this was the part of the nightmare where I would wake up.

But it was not a bad dream. It was just a bad life. I ended up at a battered women's shelter with my mother. The shelter was cold, bare and noisy. We shared a large bedroom with several other mothers and children.

I attended school on the premises and spent my afternoons attending counseling sessions. In my spare time, I learned to carve soap, which I found rather therapeutic. I missed my school and my friends but knew it was safer here, away from my father.

In the stillness of the night, I couldn't help but wonder if this was how every other little girl lived. Running from an angry, abusive alcoholic father, sleeping in shelters, getting escorted from school by the cops.

One morning, my mother shook me awake at the crack of dawn. "Get up, Christy," she urged in a loud whisper. "We need to go to the store."

The store? But we haven't left since we arrived at the shelter!

I obediently climbed out of bed and shoved my

Stories from the Oasis

feet into my shoes. Only then did I notice my mother had neatly packed our belongings, and they were at the foot of the bed. "What's going on?" I whispered.

"Not now, Christy." She grabbed my hand tightly. "Try to be quiet on your way out," she pleaded.

We stepped out into the stillness of the morning and trudged down the road. I still had the nagging feeling we weren't really going to the store.

Where is Mom really taking me?

We stopped at a payphone, and my mother asked me to stay by the sidewalk while she made a quick call. Now I really knew something was up.

Who could she be calling at this early hour?

Moments later, the puzzle pieces fell into place. An all too familiar El Camino roared to the side of the road, and my father stepped out. It had been just a few weeks since we'd seen him, but it seemed he had aged overnight. His eyes looked as though they hadn't seen an ounce of sleep. He moved toward us without a word, took our suitcases and shoved them into the back of the car.

"Come along, Christy," my mother snapped, yanking the car door open.

My heart sank. *How can my mother do this? Hadn't the point of the shelter been to keep us*

Hungry No More

away from my father? And where is he taking us? Without a word, I slid into the backseat. The vinyl felt cold against my bare legs. I stared straight ahead and prayed my father would not hurt us again.

The abuse continued, though, this time worse than before. One morning, when I was half awake, my father climbed into my bed without his clothes and rubbed up against me. "How's my little girl?" he whispered, the stench of alcohol on his breath.

I froze, horrified. His hairy arms prickled my skin as he inched toward me.

No, no! This can't be happening!

I tried to move my lips, but no words escaped. My heart thumped wildly in my chest as I silently prayed he would leave.

This sort of abuse continued for the next couple of years, along with the physical and emotional abuse. I hated to cry, as I knew it made my father happy to see me moved to tears. The easiest way to get me to shed tears was to beat my little brother. I could not stand to see my father hurt him as he had hurt me.

One evening, my father beat my brother especially bad. Each whack across his little face sent a chill up my spine. It felt as if he was ripping into my own flesh every time he struck him. Cowering

Stories from the Oasis

in the corner of the living room, I cringed as I fought back tears.

My father paused to look over at me, as if to say, "Now you gonna cry?"

I couldn't help it. The tears poured down my cheeks like water from a flowing river. "Stop it!" I screamed. "Just stop it!" I didn't care what my father thought. This was an outrage! It sickened me that my father gained pleasure from causing us pain.

My parents finally divorced when I was 10. A wave of relief washed over me when my mother broke the news. I prayed this might be the end of it for all of us. Hopefully, we could move on to a better place.

But it was not the end. One chilly night, my father pounded down the front door of our house, tore into the living room and exploded in a fit of rage. The sight of him nearly took my breath away. I had been so sure he was out of our lives! I was told that he had moved in with another woman, and it had been several weeks since we'd heard from him. I had actually started sleeping through the night for the first time in years.

My father stormed through the room like a beast in search of his prey. He grabbed my mother off the sofa by her hair.

Hungry No More

Turning to my brother and me, he sneered, "You move, you cry, I kill her. Understand?"

We nodded, terrified. My legs trembled so badly I feared I might collapse to the ground. Surely he was drunk. He was always irrational when he drank.

Please, please don't hurt my mother!

He pulled a knife from his pocket and held it to my mother's throat. He then proceeded to rape her right in front of us. My heart broke as I watched my mother, a helpless rag doll in his arms.

The knife pierced the side of her neck and blood spurted out. I feared I might faint. This was the sort of stuff horror movies were made of. Every ounce of me yearned to scream out for help, but I feared he might really kill my mother if I did. So I stood watching, helpless and terrified.

At last, my father put the knife down and sank onto the couch. Suddenly, his demeanor changed completely. A wave of sadness washed over his face as he shook his head. "I'm so sorry. I just want us to be together forever. I don't want to lose you all," he moaned, tears streaming down his face.

You're crazy. I had to bite my tongue to keep the words from escaping my lips.

Crazy! One minute you're raping my mother, the next you're telling us we should be together

STORIES FROM THE OASIS

forever? You're out of your mind!

Moments later, two cops stormed through the broken door. "Anyone home?" they called out.

Relief washed over me as they charged toward my father, guns poised. "Neighbor called, said he heard a lot of yelling over here. You want to explain?"

My father shook his head numbly and let the knife fall from his hands. He didn't need to explain. It was just as it looked — a drunken man abusing his ex-wife. The cops arrested my father and took him away.

We huddled together and cried for several minutes after he left. My mother pressed her palm to her neck where the knife had stabbed her. It felt like that knife stabbed us all that night — stabbed a hole right through our hearts. I desperately hoped this would be the end of my father.

My father moved to Tennessee shortly after he got out of jail. We tried to resume a normal life, but none of us really knew how. I trudged through school in a state of numbness. My mother worked three jobs to put a roof over our heads and food in our mouths. Though things were still tight, I was grateful that we no longer went hungry. No longer did we have to scramble for scraps of food under the table, while my father dined like a king.

Hungry No More

One evening, a wonderful man stepped into my life. He came to the strip club a few times and often engaged in small talk with me while I worked. He appeared to have little interest in the other strippers, unlike most of the other gawking patrons. His interest in me seemed genuine, and he often lingered to chat after the club closed.

"Why do you like me?" I asked him one day, perplexed.

"I just like talking to you. You're real. You're not like the other girls that work here," he replied. "I want to get to know you more."

We began casually dating, and I realized how genuinely kind he was. Never in my life had a man treated me with such respect. He truly seemed to care about *me*. I was flattered but baffled. Considering my past and present life, I didn't much feel I deserved his attention.

My personal life continued to spiral out of control. I became even more heavily involved with cocaine. While harmless fun at first, it was now the center of my universe. I nearly panicked if I couldn't get my fix. Inside, I was crumbling.

One day, in early October, my uncle came to town and approached me at the club. "We need to talk, Christy," he said, his voice low and urgent. "You can't go on living like this. Your mom says

Stories from the Oasis

you're a mess. You've gotta get out of here. Please consider moving to New Mexico to stay with me while you screw your head back on straight."

His words hung heavily on me as the night went on. Before my shift was even over, I hung up my towel and abruptly walked home, teetering on my heels as I trudged down the road. I hadn't a clue what I was going to do next, but I knew I needed help.

Perhaps my uncle's suggestion is the ticket out of this dead end life.

My aunt showed up at my apartment a while later and drove me out of town. It was nearly 2 a.m.; there was hardly a car on the road as we sped through the night. I hadn't told a soul I was leaving, not even my boyfriend. A mixture of fear and excitement mounted in my veins as we drove. *A new town, a new life. What will become of me in New Mexico?*

To everyone's surprise, including my own, I was able to stop using drugs when I arrived in New Mexico. It was hard and not without temptation, but I was able to control my impulses. The drinking continued, but this didn't faze my family in the least.

I found work at a craft store and enjoyed being in a positive environment for the first time in my

Hungry No More

life. I missed my boyfriend and thought of him often but knew I had made the right decision. My aunt and uncle's close watch provided the accountability I needed to stay on the right track.

Thanksgiving rolled around, and the air turned crisp. One morning, my uncle handed me the telephone as I came downstairs for breakfast. I wondered who could be calling me. I hadn't forwarded my information to anyone and hadn't made any new friends in town.

"Hello?" I asked hesitantly.

"Christy? It's Ben. Where have you been? I've been looking all over for you!"

My heart caught in my throat. "How on earth did you find me?" I croaked.

"It's a long story," he replied, his voice tender. "I'll tell you later. Right now, I just want to see you. I miss you. I was thinking of coming for Christmas. Would that be okay?"

My heart soared at the thought of seeing him again. But I didn't want to appear too excited. "I'm sorry I left without telling you, Ben," I replied. "I just had to get my life cleaned up, and I didn't want anyone to stop me from leaving. I've been doing great. I'd love to see you."

Even as I hung up, I wondered whether he'd really come. El Paso was a 600-mile drive.

Stories from the Oasis

Would he really show up?

As promised, Ben showed up on Christmas. I was more than happy to see his smiling face. He wrapped me in his arms as I filled him in on the details of my new life. He didn't seem angry, as I feared he might be, but instead listened intently. When the weekend was over and it was time for him to leave, he whispered, "Christy, I love you."

I gulped.

Did he just say the L-word? But we've only known each other a few months! "Thanks," I muttered, not quite ready to return the powerful statement.

"Move back to Texas," he pleaded. "We need to be together."

I shook my head. "I can't. I'm doing so well here."

"Please. You don't have to go back to your old ways. We can start a new life together." His eyes were pleading.

I sighed. "I'll think about it."

We continued to date long distance for several weeks, but it put a strain on both of us. Again, he begged me to come back to Texas. "I'm going to come visit you next week. And if I leave without you this time, it's over for us," he said firmly.

My heart sank. I desperately wanted to be with

Hungry No More

Ben, but I wasn't sure I could face everyone in my hometown. So many bad memories lay there. What if I slipped back into my old habits or ran into my old friends?

Ben showed up again, as promised, begging me to go home with him. At first I refused, but on the day he was to leave, I quickly changed my mind. "I'll go," I conceded and ran to gather my belongings. I knew my uncle would be terribly disappointed in me, but I simply could not let Ben go.

We returned to Texas, and I moved into his house. I contacted my uncle to let him know I had left. He was furious and tried to convince me our relationship would never last. "You've made a very foolish move, Christy," he told me angrily. "Don't contact me again."

"I'm sorry," I mumbled.

Ben and I became engaged shortly after I moved in with him and married in July. I was elated when I became pregnant five months after our wedding. With a wonderful husband and a baby on the way, surely the emptiness I had struggled to fill all these years would finally disappear.

The moment I laid eyes on my precious daughter, I felt an unexplainable love like nothing I'd ever experienced. Suddenly, I was both thrilled and terrified.

Stories from the Oasis

How can I parent a little girl at the age of 20, when I am still a child myself? Years of bottled up pain, confusion and hurt overtook me as I held her in my arms, suddenly feeling the weight of her tiny frame.

"You were born to the worst person," I whispered, tears streaming down my cheeks. "I can't take care of you." At that moment, I truly hated my parents. I hated them for not defending me, for abandoning me, for abusing me, for misunderstanding me. It was all so unfair! A deep, dark hole filled my heart as I cried, tears splashing onto her silky pink cheeks.

One morning, at 2 a.m., I flew out of bed and shook my husband. "You've got to commit me!" I screamed. "I'm going crazy!"

He rubbed his eyes groggily. "What are you talking about?"

"Ever since I had this baby, I feel like I'm going crazy! I can't do this!"

"Go back to sleep, Christy. You'll be okay," my ever-calm husband replied, rolling over.

I sat up in bed, sobbing uncontrollably. It was as if a floodgate of emotions had opened, and there was no turning back. That little girl under the table pining for a scrap of food was suddenly before me, crying, too.

Hungry No More

Why me? I cried out to no one in particular. I did not believe in God. I had heard many people talk about him growing up but had refused to believe that a God could really let a little girl suffer as I had. If there was a God, he was supposed to be loving and compassionate, not indifferent.

Ben and I had three more children, two daughters and a son. I sank into a deep, terrible 10-year depression. Each morning, I awoke in tears, and each night, I fell asleep crying into my pillow. Though I always made sure my children's physical needs were taken care of, I was checked out emotionally, too depressed to be in tune with their lives.

September 11th hit, and I spent the entire day huddled on the couch, my eyes glued to the TV watching the twin towers falling in billows of smoke. "What sort of a horrible world do we live in?" I moaned to my husband. "How can we raise children in this world?" Suddenly, life had no meaning. I felt emptier than ever before.

Just when it seemed I'd hit rock bottom, my husband sustained a work-related injury that left him paralyzed from the waist down. I was forced to return to work, and we moved into my sister's basement. Depression overwhelmed me.

One week, my friend from work called to invite

Stories from the Oasis

me to church. "God put you on my heart, and I thought you might want to come to church with me tomorrow," she said hopefully.

"God put me on your heart?" I stifled a laugh. "Sorry, not interested."

The following week, my friend showed up at my house and invited me to church again. This time, she asked me in front of my oldest daughter, Aubrey.

The minute Aubrey heard the word "church," her eyes lit up. "Please, Mom? Can we go?" she begged.

I shook my head vehemently. "No," I said firmly.

My daughter went into her room and threw herself on her bed, sobbing. "Please, Mom! Please let us go to church!" she begged between her tears.

I had never seen my daughter so emphatic about something. At last, I relented. "All right, we'll go next Sunday. Are you happy now?"

She wiped her tears and sniffed. "Yes."

Sunday rolled around, and I reluctantly climbed out of bed. To my surprise, my daughter had gotten all of her siblings dressed, groomed and fed. Four anxious pairs of eyes stared back at me as I stepped out of my bedroom. "Ready, Mom?"

I sighed. "Ready as I'll ever be." I tried to

Hungry No More

muster a shred of enthusiasm as we drove to church that morning. *I'm doing it for the kids. I don't need to go to church and hear this baloney. But I'll go for them.*

The church, Abundant Living Faith Center, was enormous! We snuck into the back and sat down quietly.

I turned my eyes to the front of the room where the pastor stood to begin his sermon. *Just grin and bear it, and you'll be out of here in an hour.*

"This morning, we are going to talk about a very special woman in the Bible named Esther," the pastor began. "Esther was a beautiful young woman who obeyed God, despite difficult circumstances." He went on to speak about Esther, who overcame much adversity and eventually became the queen. The story was especially fascinating.

"Just as Esther, you were all born for such a time as this," the pastor concluded. "You may have walked into church this morning with a heavy burden on your shoulders. You may have an ugly, hurtful past. You may be sitting here wondering what on earth your purpose is. I can assure you, you each have one. God has a special plan for each of your lives, even if it does not feel like it today."

Sudden tears sprang to my eyes as he spoke. It

Stories from the Oasis

seemed he was looking straight at me, directing his message just to me! *How does he know my life? Did my friend tell him I was coming? Did she tell him to preach this message just for me this morning? This is all a bit too eerie!*

I approached my friend after church. "Did you tell the pastor I was coming this morning?" I hissed. "It was as if he knew my whole life story!"

My friend laughed and shook her head. "It's called the Holy Spirit, Christy. God knew you needed to hear that message this morning. I've never personally spoken to the pastor in my life. But it was no coincidence. God wanted you here this morning."

I was not convinced. Surely someone must have known my story and shared it with the pastor. His message had been tailored just for me!

Fascinated by this strange "coincidence," I returned to Abundant Living Faith Center the following week without my children. I snuck into the back pew and hunkered down so the pastor would not see me. I did not want him to know I was there.

A man in front of me turned around to say hello. "Are you all right?" he asked.

"Shh! I don't want the pastor to see me!" I whispered loudly.

Hungry No More

"Okaaay," the man replied with a shrug.

Once again, the pastor preached a powerful, moving message, which seemed as if he had custom written it just for me. And once again, I found myself sobbing quietly as his words moved into my heart. He spoke about a loving God who was near to the brokenhearted, compassionate and kind. Suddenly, I knew what was missing in my life. I wanted a relationship with the God he spoke of! I wanted to confess my sins, so I could live a life of freedom and experience his love!

When the pastor asked if anyone would like to come forward to receive Christ as his or her Savior, I nearly leapt up and flew to the front of the room.

Tears streamed down my cheeks as I prayed with a woman in the front to receive Christ into my heart. I felt a warmth and peace like I had never experienced in my life as I uttered a simple prayer that would change my life forever. No longer would I go through life as a wounded victim without a purpose.

I was a child of God, a precious woman loved by the king! He had a special purpose for my life and had waited patiently many years for me to walk into his arms.

"Is there anything you would like prayer for?" the woman asked kindly.

Stories from the Oasis

I nodded and wiped my tears. "My husband has been paralyzed for the past few months. He needs approval for a surgery that could help him walk again."

The woman prayed a simple but passionate prayer, asking the Lord to heal my husband and allow us to find the right doctors to do his surgery. I had goose bumps when we opened our eyes. "I'll be praying for you, dear," she said, squeezing my shoulder.

"Thank you so much!" I nearly shouted. I felt like dancing down the aisle as I returned to my seat. Suddenly, my friend's words made sense.

God had wanted me in this church at this very moment so that I could give my heart to him. How amazing!

The very next morning, I received a phone call from my husband's doctor. "We would like to do the surgery on your husband," he told me.

My heart soared. "You're kidding!" I cried. "This is wonderful news!" I was blown away that my prayers had been answered so quickly. It felt as if a floodgate of blessings had been opened up from heaven and poured down on me. I felt more hopeful than I had in years.

Two weeks later, my husband went in for his much-awaited surgery. Thirty minutes after the

Hungry No More

surgery was completed, he was able to walk again. The doctors were amazed, as was I. "Thank you, Lord!" I cried out once again. God had healed my husband. What a miracle!

The next few weeks were a whirlwind of emotions as I grew in my relationship with the Lord. For a woman who hadn't even believed God existed growing up, I had a lot to learn. At every turn, I was continually amazed at the things that he showed me. I found that if I truly sought him, through reading my Bible and praying, he would open my mind and my heart to understand his character and give me the strength to obey him and trust him.

Ten years of depression were replaced with a heart full of hope and a spring in my step. I no longer had a desire to use foul language. God healed my mouth overnight. He also spoke to me about my alcoholism.

One afternoon, I strongly felt the urge to pour out all my alcohol. I went to the cupboard and took out all my bottles. There were nearly 100 of them! One by one, I opened them and poured them down the sink drain, praising the Lord that I no longer had the desire to drink. I now had something much stronger to fill me up: Jesus himself!

We moved from El Paso, Texas, to Rockwall,

Stories from the Oasis

Texas. My children and I began attending Oasis Church, where we were welcomed right away. After settling in, we began volunteering for the youth program. I was delighted to see them thrive in their new relationships with God, as well. My husband, however, remained skeptical. Despite having seen God perform a miracle on his body, he wasn't sure church and God were really for him.

On Valentine's Day a year prior, I was shocked to learn I had seven tumors on my thyroid gland. After performing surgery to remove them, the doctor found they were only cysts and was able to successfully drain them. I was thankful for my clean bill of health. However, a year later on Valentine's Day again, I learned the tumors had returned. I prayed God would heal me but had to put my health on the back burner as my life was moving at a whirlwind pace.

One morning at church, Pastor Barney greeted me and asked me about my husband. I explained that he was currently working in California and that we did not get to see him often. I also let him know that he was not a believer.

"Can I pray for you and your family?" Pastor Barney asked kindly.

I bobbed my head up and down. "Thank you. That would be wonderful."

Hungry No More

That morning, Pastor Barney asked the entire church to pray for my family. I was so honored that my new church family had embraced us so openly. My fervent prayer was that one day my husband would join our new family, as well.

At last, one Sunday morning, my husband agreed to go to church with us. He gave his heart to the Lord that morning, and we all rejoiced. We were now complete as a family in our relationships with Christ.

My heart sang, knowing I would see my dear husband in heaven. God had answered my prayers and the prayers of my precious new friends at Oasis Church. For the first time in my life, I truly realized the power of prayer.

As my relationship with my husband began to thrive, I revisited the issue of the tumors. I knew I could not ignore them any longer but did not know what step to take next. Should I see another doctor or leave the healing up to God?

After all, he had miraculously opened my husband's eyes to the truths of the Bible. Surely he could heal my tumors.

I prayed and felt God wanted me to confide in Pastor Barney, his wife, Cindy, and their son, Lindsey, about the tumors. I kept my burden to myself, however, for several more weeks.

Stories from the Oasis

One morning, my daughter returned from church flushed and excited. "Mom, God told me that Lindsey is supposed to pray for you!" she said breathlessly.

I raised my eyebrows. I had not told my daughter about the tumors. At that moment, I knew I needed to obey God and tell my pastor and his family about my situation. Immediately, I picked up the phone and asked Pastor Barney for prayer.

"Is there anything else I can pray for?" Pastor Barney asked after praying over my tumors.

I paused. "Yes, there is. I still harbor quite a bit of resentment and bitterness toward my parents for my childhood." Tears burned my eyes as I shared with him how difficult it had been to forgive my parents for the way they had treated me growing up.

Pastor Barney prayed again for me, and I then called Lindsey, who prayed with me, as well. Feeling lighter than I had in months, I hung up and smiled. It felt good to confide in someone. Perhaps it was the first step toward complete physical and emotional healing.

A few weeks later, while sitting in church with my daughter, I received a call from Lindsey. He had gone with Pastor Barney and several kids from the school of ministry to Florida for a revival event.

Hungry No More

When I answered my phone, he sounded nearly frantic. "Christy, I need to pray for you right now!" he burst out. "The pastor told us to call those we know who have tumors, and God will heal them!"

I sucked in my breath. "Wow! That's amazing!" I replied, trying to keep my excitement to a loud whisper. "Go for it!"

Lindsey prayed for me over the phone, and I began to quietly sob. "Do you still feel the tumor?" Lindsey asked me.

"Yes," I whispered. "Keep praying!"

"Touch it!" Lindsey commanded and continued to pray.

I put my finger on the lump, which was roughly the size of an Adam's apple. Slowly, I felt it began to deflate. I screamed aloud and began crying uncontrollably. People in church began to look around and stare at me, but I didn't care. God had healed my tumors! It was truly a miracle! At that moment, I was reminded not only of the miraculous power of prayer but of another miracle: stumbling into Oasis Church.

At last, I had found a place to call home, a place where I was loved, accepted and truly cared about.

A picture of Jesus on the cross remained etched in my mind as I drove home that evening. If Jesus

Stories from the Oasis

could forgive the worst of sinners, surely he could help me forgive my parents. "Lord, help me!" I cried out. "I want to be free of this resentment. Help me to trust in you and forgive my parents for the hurt and pain they have caused me."

In the stillness of the evening, I felt God speak to me. He told me that the tumors were roots of anger and bitterness toward my parents and that I was born to the perfect parents, whether or not it seemed like it as a child. "I was always there with you, Christy," I felt him say. "Now go and make amends with those you harbor bitterness toward."

That evening, as tears steamed down my cheeks, I wrote each of my parents a letter, telling them that I loved them and wanted to restore my relationship with them. My fingers shook as I put pen to paper, wondering how they would react after years of strain. I prayed that God might open their hearts someday, too.

Over the next few weeks, I wrote letters to others whom I had harbored resentment toward during my life. I felt wonderfully free, knowing I was obeying God and making the step toward restoring relationships.

As the months passed, my relationship with my husband and children flourished.

My daughter announced she wanted to attend

Hungry No More

a school of ministry, while my son learned to worship the Lord with his musical talent.

I fell in love with Psalms 112: "How joyful are those who fear the Lord and delight in obeying his commands. Their children will be successful … an entire generation of godly people will be blessed …"

Over and over again, I thanked the Lord for restoring my family and for causing me to walk into Oasis Church that wonderful morning. A simple invitation from a friend had changed my family's lives forever.

This past Mother's Day, my husband flew in from out of state just to take me to dinner. It was a wonderful, romantic move that touched my heart. Once again, I was reminded of what a wonderful man God brought into my life.

As I gazed over the dinner table into my husband's warm brown eyes, I couldn't help but smile. "You know, our relationship reminds me of my relationship with God," I told him. "Even in the depths of my troubled life, you pursued me, you sought me out. I couldn't understand why you drove hundreds of miles just to find me and loved me for who I was. God has done the same thing in my life. He quietly pursued me and did not give up on me, even when I denied his existence. And now

Stories from the Oasis

my relationship with him is stronger than ever. I'm so thankful."

My husband squeezed my hand and smiled back. God had greatly blessed his trucking business in the past few months, and though this meant him traveling more, he never ceased to make our family a priority. "I knew you were special from the moment I laid eyes on you, Christy," he told me gently. "I guess I should thank you for not giving up on me, either. I am eternally grateful for your persistent prayers. I can't imagine not having you, or God, in my life."

My heart felt lighter than ever as I kissed my husband goodbye that evening. I thought, once again, of that little girl under the table, desperate for a scrap of food. No longer did I have to live hungry. I had found purpose in Christ; he alone filled me up! He had not only restored me but blessed me, as well. And that was far more than my heart could ever have asked for.

2
Nueva Cada Dia
(New Each Day)
The Story of Jan
Written by Anne Johnson

"Oh, God, please spare my life!" I wiped my straight, black hair from my eyes. Blood? I had to get out. I pressed against the car door with all my might. The stench of smoke filled the air.

My chest hurt as I breathed. I could not get enough air; it was like breathing through a coffee straw. I felt more blood trickle down my face. Like holding a friend's hand, fear nestled close and apprehended my heart.

In my mind, I was 6 again. My mom lay on the living room floor, her swollen face buried in the green shag rug.

"Ese danos," she said in her native tongue.

"Sorry, Mommy. It's bad," I said.

"Just clean it off."

I tried once more to stop the blood. The stab wound in her back was deep. I was used to cleaning my mom's injuries that were inflicted by my dad, but this time, I needed help.

"Mommy, the blood keeps coming." I pressed the cotton ball against her back. She didn't wince. She never did.

"Bien," she groaned. "Recuerde, no diga cualiquier persona sobre esto."

"I know," I assured her. "I remember. I won't tell anyone about this."

I watched her put her tattered floral blouse

back on. She turned to face me. I didn't gasp when I saw her bruised face. Her dark complexion hid most of her bruises, but when they were new, they had a bright blue tinge to them.

My mother and father held tight to their Hispanic traditions, almost to the point of defiance. They had lived in Texas for years but never learned to speak or write English. However, as a child, I was forced to meld my heritage with my current surroundings. But I was not alone. The majority of children I went to school and grew up with were also a part of this multicultural melting pot. I had grown up being my parents' voice in the community, and it wasn't about to change.

My mother grabbed her keys and purse. I jumped up. "Please, take me, too," I begged.

She held the front door open. I ran out, hoping never to see that two-bedroom prison again.

Suddenly, I returned to my frightening predicament.

"Prison. I'm in prison." I shoved against the car door again. The reality of the pain in my arm helped alleviate the painful memories of earlier years.

The pungent odor of burnt rubber permeated the car. I couldn't see the passenger side of the car; the roof lay between me and the other seat.

Nueva Cada Dia

I heard voices outside. "Help me, please! Somebody, please help!" I screamed.

I had cried for help all of my life. I bawled when my mother drove us back to our home after we had spent a week away from my father. She had threatened to press charges and expose his abuse to the local Catholic church we sporadically attended. The physical abuse stopped, but my father's drunken rages were at times more dreadful. The emotional scars tore deeper into the core of our family, driving a wedge between us.

"It will be different this time," my mother said. "He said he was sorry."

I refused to look at her. I stared out the window. My way to safety began to narrow as we headed back to the slums. Like a hamster on a squeaky wheel, we were returning to our captor. I clenched my small fists, my fingernails digging into my palms. I didn't want to go back. I wanted to run away, but there was nowhere to go. I never talked with anyone about the abuse at home or my dad's alcohol consumption. I figured my life was no different than anyone else's. But in my heart, I wanted out. I wanted release from the fear that consumed me and the hopelessness that wrapped around my life like a python around its prey's neck.

Stories from the Oasis

I yanked at my seatbelt, but it stubbornly refused to release its lifesaving hold on me. Finally, reluctantly, the tab slid from the buckle. "Dong, dong," the seatbelt chimed, warning me that I was no longer safely fastened in, as I frantically squirmed toward the window. Glass shards tore at my shirt as I pressed my body through the car window. I could feel the sharp points of the snarled glass stick into my arms and belly. My head cleared the door, and I sucked in a breath of humid air. I felt the tightness in my chest flee. A drop of blood landed on a piece of glass. Its crimson hue gave the glass a new light. A new perspective.

**

"Come on, class sucks. Let's ditch and go to my house."

I looked around the schoolyard. There was a sea of black-haired children that ebbed and flowed before me. The recess workers were once again busy separating a brawl. I glared at the girls doing tricks on the monkey bars. Their high-pitched thrills grated at my raw nerves.

"Okay, let's go."

Together, we made for the corner of the schoolyard. We pretended to play chase as we ran

Nueva Cada Dia

along the fence. The tightness in my stomach increased as the bell rang, and my friend ducked out of sight behind a tree. I watched the flurry of children rush toward the school.

"Come on," Maria hissed.

I hesitated and then took the plunge. For 13 years, I had watched my father drink to the point of passing out. If he didn't pass out, then he would fight with my mom. I sought shelter under my covers and hoped the ragged blanket would protect me. My heart was ripped in two every time the arguing began. I feared for my mother's safety yet was relieved I wasn't the focus of my dad's anger. The bitterness in my heart grew in the fertile ground of fear that surrounded my life.

"Gee, did you have to cut it so close?" Maria asked.

We sat under the shade of the tree until the second bell rang. Once the noise from the playground vanished, we hurried toward Maria's house.

"What are we going to do?" I asked.

"I don't know. What do you want to do?"

"Got any new games?"

Maria nodded. "I got a great one."

We pushed the broken screen door aside and walked into the house. I kicked my sandals off and

Stories from the Oasis

followed Maria to her room. I had been in her home many times, and the layout of it was no different than mine or any other home on the block.

I plopped down on the lower bunk and curled my feet under me. "Don't get too comfortable. We're going back outside."

Maria fished through her older sister's desk drawer. She mumbled about how cluttered the drawer was then held up the trophy of her expedition. I looked at the plastic bag and then at Maria. "And we're going to do what with that?"

"Smoke it."

"Smoke it?"

"Yeah," she said. "It's pot."

I hesitated again. Maria lowered the bag and her eyes. Her bottom lip puckered, and her shoulders sagged. I didn't want to hurt her feelings. I needed her friendship and acceptance. And I wanted to have fun. "Okay. How do we do it?"

Outside, we shared a joint. With each drag, I felt the bitterness in my heart drop like leaves in the fall. We looked up at the wispy white clouds. I imagined myself floating among them, jumping from one to the other, not apprehensive of the danger of falling but free.

Nueva Cada Dia

***

It had been but a moment in time, but as my body hung out the crushed car window, I relived the start of my addiction to drugs. I pressed my legs hard against the seat of the car. My body thudded onto the road. I felt the hot cement beneath me and heard the crunch of glass. My eyelids were heavy. I tried to pry my eyes open. Was this a dream? I tried to remember where I was or what I had been doing. But all I felt was the world spinning around me. My face grew warm, and then everything went dark.

***

For four years, I was able to hide my drug use from my parents. Throughout junior high, my dependency grew. Instead of being a game or recreational, drugs became my life. They were my method of survival. I was exposed to many forms of drugs and how to best use them to cover up their side effects. I learned to snort cocaine if the alcohol made me wobbly. I smoked pot to calm myself if I was too hyper. Visine took the red out of my eyes. Deodorant kept my hands dry, and perfume covered any smell that hung on me.

Stories from the Oasis

My parents received a multitude of truancy reports, but because they only spoke and read Spanish, they never knew about my drug use. At the end of each semester, I would beg my teachers to let me do extra credit to pass each class. They did.

By the time I was 17, I was drinking and doing drugs daily. I skipped school to get high or joined my classmates in rolling up a dollar bill and snorting a row of cocaine off my school desk while the teacher's back was turned. It seemed every week there were dog raids. The word was whispered from one corner of the school to another. It was easy to fool the police and the K-9s.

I remember the dogs sniffing my backpack, and though I wasn't asking God for help, I hoped I had hid my drugs well enough. Concealed in plastic bags or wrapped in gym clothes, I would hold my bag open and allow the dog's wet, slimy nose to prowl around. There were times I hadn't been able to sell my goods. I would scamper out the back doors of the school, evading teachers and police, while seeking refuge behind the large Catholic church adjacent to our school property.

I watched in horror as police handcuffed students and took them away. I would clench my jaw and hear my heartbeat drumming in my ears.

Nueva Cada Dia

Other kids would snicker and point as our classmates were led outside and shoved into the patrol car. Our teachers would fight to win back control of the classrooms. I forced myself to sit through class, and when the bell rang, I rushed off to the bathroom to snort cocaine to quiet my nerves.

Once, when a friend and I were at the post office, we saw a familiar face on the FBI's most wanted list. Instead of scaring us into changing our life habits, we found it a thrill. The external danger factor fueled my internal fear. As terror mounted within me, my drug intake escalated.

Though the drugs deadened my resentment toward my mom and anger at my dad, I lived in fear of being discovered. I dreaded my parents' response. I didn't want to be kicked out of my house, and I didn't want the police to arrest me. My desire to remain in the haze of reality deepened my dependency. It took more pot to gain the same mental freedom. In high school, I began to sell drugs. I would sell drugs to anyone. I was not concerned with the effects drugs had on anyone else, nor did I care if I sold drugs to children. I needed my fix, and that was all that mattered. I would take or try anything I was offered, with the exception of intravenous drugs. To me, that was going too far.

I reached a point in my drug abuse where I was

Stories from the Oasis

admired by friends for being able to "handle" more than anyone else. I had learned the more you could drink or smoke without getting sick, the cooler you were. At parties, I could out drink all the girls and many of the guys. My tolerance was my success and a flawed form of self-esteem. When I wasn't high or drunk, I would pray that someone would save me. I wanted out, but no one listened. No one heard me.

***

"Help me!" I tried to scream, but only a whimper came out. I wanted to move. *I need to get up.* But my body did not respond. I heard the whiz of cars going by and a dog barking in the distance. I wasn't dead, but why couldn't I move? "God. Please. I'm... I'm sorry."

Strength coursed through my body like a spring runoff down a mountainside. I pressed my arms into the ground. From the push-up position, I maneuvered to my knees and raised my head. Was I on a merry-go-round? I kept my eyes closed, all the while hearing people's voices. I didn't scream for help this time but prayed again. "Please, God, help me."

The spinning stopped, and I rose to my feet. I

Nueva Cada Dia

opened my eyes. I stood in a sea of glass. There were people staring at me on both sides of the street. Their faces were pale, and their eyes wider than a full moon. I turned around and sucked in a breath of air. There before me was my car. A telephone pole had split the car in half. The roof caved in. If I were an observer, I too would think the person who crawled out of that wreck was a ghost.

In that moment, I recalled the other time in my life when the people around me thought I was some sort of ghoul.

***

"It has to be this way, don't you see?" Antonio declared.

I stepped closer to him, my chest pressed against his. "No!" I shouted.

Though the music blared, everyone at the party stopped their drinking and snorting to look at the two of us. Antonio's olive skin reddened. I saw his jaw tighten and knew I had gone too far. He turned and stomped out of the door.

I looked around the room. "What?" I hollered. No one answered me. They just stared, joints held in mid-position, beer bottles inches from the consumers' mouths. I hated everyone staring at me. I

Stories from the Oasis

felt as if they all knew about my ... I fled the room.

I found Antonio on the front steps. "I know you're right."

"I'll go with you," he said, placing his arm around me.

I shuttered at his touch. I no longer felt comfort and loathed the choice I felt forced to make.

A week later, I sat in Doctor Tilley's office, listening to him prattle on about how I had choices. Anger burned in me like a smoldering cigarette.

"You can place the child up for adoption, or perhaps your folks would help you."

"No," I declared. "I've made up my mind." I proceeded to sign the papers.

Dr. Tilley nodded and led me to the exam room. The nurse gave me some medication that was supposed to deaden the pain, but my drug history caused me to be tolerant. Excruciating pain radiated from my abdomen into my groin. I felt a warm flush sensation and knew it would be seconds before I succumbed to darkness. However, I never passed out. Instead, I suffered the removal of life from my body while I was awake.

The nurse and doctor lifted me into a wheelchair. As they pushed me through the waiting room toward my friend, the other patients stared at me. No one made eye contact. One lady shook

Nueva Cada Dia

her head back and forth while making some sort of hissing sound under her breath. I wanted to die. I felt as if part of me had died. My friend helped me into the car and took me to a motel. I spent the next few nights in a drunken stupor, enduring excruciating pain if I slept too long in between shots of whiskey and beer.

Day and night, I was haunted by that woman's face in the waiting room and the disapproval of her avoiding gaze. I couldn't close my eyes without seeing and hearing my parents' horror-filled cries as they grieved the grandchild they would never know. "Oh, God, what have I done?"

After the abortion, I hated Antonio and myself. It was then that I began to cry out to God. "Please, I know I will spend eternity in hell for all I have done, but help me now. I don't want to live like this anymore," I begged. Again and again, I pleaded to God.

Maybe it was a change in attitude, but I began to notice occurrences in my life only divine intervention could explain. One night, I was dressed and waiting for my friends to pick me up for a party. I paced around my small bedroom. The carpet in my room was thin, so the sound of my heels clicked on the floor. My dad pounded on the wall from out in the living room. I flopped down on the

Stories from the Oasis

bed. "Where are you guys?" I muttered.

I woke to more pounding on the wall. My dad was yelling for me to answer the phone. I stomped into the living room, grabbed the receiver and went out onto the front porch. In the darkness, I all but screamed, "I'm waiting!"

"Jess," Darra cried. "Oh my …"

"Darra? What's wrong?"

"A shot … the house."

"What shot? What house? Darra, calm down."

"Right as we were pulling up!" Darra wailed.

I could hear my other friends in the background. I wanted to wrap my arms around Darra and comfort her. Or choke her so she would tell me what had happened. She had been with me during my… I didn't want to think about it. "What are you talking about?" I demanded, ashamed at how angry I sounded.

"We were just checking out the action," Darra whimpered. "Then we were going to come get you."

I heard her sniffle. "Go on," I coaxed.

"We were across the street when a black van drove by and began shooting. Someone… someone inside fell."

"What?"

"We didn't stay around," she sniffed. "Jess, it

Nueva Cada Dia

could have been one of us."

She was right. Two weeks later, I was home again waiting for my friend, Gea, to pick me up for a party. For some reason, she decided to pick up our drugs first. When she pulled up to the curb, a man jumped out from around the side of the house and began shooting at the passenger seat. The bullets piercing the metal of the door sounded like an ice pick plunging into a coffee can. Screaming, Gea slammed her foot to the floor. Tires squealed, and she screamed in terror. That was the seat — the same seat I would have been in if Gea had picked me up first, as we had planned.

A few weeks after the shootings, a friend's mom asked me if I would be her receptionist. I was almost 18 and needed work. I also knew I needed to change the way I was living my life. My father had quit drinking because he had become very ill from the side effects of alcohol. I knew the path I was on would lead me in the same direction.

I accepted the receptionist job, and every week my boss, Hanna, would invite me to church. I wanted to keep my job, so I went. She convinced my parents to join with her and send me to the private Christian school her daughter attended. I was able to graduate with the help of Hanna and merciful teachers. Though I gained new friendships,

Stories from the Oasis

drugs remained a part of my life.

An unfamiliar seed began to germinate within my heart, however. I continued to work for Hanna and go to church with her, but my reason for going changed. I began to hunger for a better understanding of God and the role he wanted to play in my life. From the pulpit, I learned about God's love, mercy, grace and forgiveness. One Sunday, as I was half dozing during the sermon, the pastor concluded with, "We must be willing to surrender everything to God."

I still don't know if it was the closing music that jolted me into complete awareness or the impossible challenge he had just issued. Something began to burn inside me. I had never known a feeling like this before. It seemed like hope was beginning to fill my heart. I went home, closed the door to my room, grabbed the dust-covered, black Bible off the nightstand and began to read. I couldn't get enough. This book that used to strike me as religious and boring began to intrigue me. I felt a strong peace fill my chest as I read the words. I hammered Hanna with questions, attended church whenever the doors were open and became addicted to God.

I pulled away from the friends who I had partied with all my life, except the man I was involved

Nueva Cada Dia

with physically. When I stumbled across the truth in God's word about sexual purity, I told my boyfriend, "We either marry or split. I'm not fornicating anymore."

To my amazement, Jose agreed to marriage. Fear that once apprehended my life melted away like ice cream on a sidewalk. Though I wasn't convinced of my eternal destination, I believed for the rest of my natural life that I would be safe.

I asked Hanna to pray for me, for I spent the weekends in bondage to old behavior. I asked her to join me in praying for my complete deliverance from drugs and alcohol. Our accountability toward one another was a key ingredient to my success in breaking free from the bondage of drug addiction.

***

Now, here I stood in the center of the street, my car split in two and not a soul willing to help me. I fell to the ground. Not because of a physical reason, but because God had seen fit to save me. Not just today, but 2,000 years ago, when his son died on the cross for my sins. All my atrocious sins — the drugs, the lies and the abortion — were all gone. What remained was a sense of safety and

Stories from the Oasis

love. I felt tears begin to sting my eyes. As they splashed down my face, I began to cry.

Right there in the street, I prayed. "God, I've done a lot of really bad things. I'm through trying to figure this out all alone. I need you. I need your love and your strength. Please fill me with your light and walk with me every step of the way."

I confessed all my sins to God. I admitted my need for a Savior, and I asked for his forgiveness. A warm blanket wrapped around me. I felt a gentle voice whisper, "Everything will be all right."

"Oh, God, thank you," I whispered.

What I had perceived as an imaginary blanket and an illusionary voice had been real. I rested my head, cradled in the lap of a woman three times my age. She softly stroked my black hair, all the while reassuring me help was on the way. But help had already arrived. God had apprehended me. My Redeemer and Savior had come. I no longer feared for my life, present or eternal.

I walked away from the car wreck I should have died in with a scratch on my ankle and head and a pair of lost shoes. But I gained hope, peace and joy. Since that day, my life has never been the same. No drugs, no fear, only love. God has shown me that the path to true fulfillment and joy is

Nueva Cada Dia

found only in him, in his presence. Life is beautiful. His mercies are new every morning.

"It is of the Lord's mercies that we are not consumed, because his compassions fail not. They are new every morning; great is thy faithfulness." (Lamentations 3:22-23)

3
Rebel Boy
The Story of Matthew
Written by Peggy Thompson

"You gonna keep lyin' to me?"

Her voice was shrill and so loud, I could hear it out on the street in front of our house.

Running up the path, I took the front stairs two at a time.

"You been lyin' to me."

The sound of breaking glass along with the screaming made me cautious, and I opened the front door slowly, carefully.

"No! I'm telling you the truth!"

As I edged my way inside the door, I spotted my father taking cover behind an overstuffed armchair. My mother was poised in the doorway between the living room and the dining room. She had picked up a glass pitcher from the sideboard and was getting ready to throw it at him.

"Mama! Don't do that!" I hadn't intended to scream so loudly.

Hurrying to her side, my eyes pleading with her, I lowered my voice. "Mama, enough. Please stop."

Quickly, I positioned myself between her and the target — my father. With one hand on her shoulder, I reached out with the other and took the glass pitcher from her.

Her chest was heaving with exertion and rivulets of perspiration were running down her face.

Stories from the Oasis

My father got up from behind the chair and slowly walked toward us. His dark brows drew together over eyes that were equally dark. He was so angry that they seemed to glint with sparks, and he stared intensely at my mother with his hands balled into fists at his sides.

"Matthew, your mama is acting crazy again."

He never laid a hand on her, but he was so upset that his hands shook as he reached up and ran his fingers through his thick, black hair.

As he stood there, Mama spat at him in disgust and turned away. He quickly sidestepped out of her line of fire.

At age 14, this was an all-too-common scene at home. After our move from Montevideo, Uruguay, to Salinas, my mother stopped going to church. My younger sister and I were quick to follow in her footsteps. Everything seemed to go downhill after that.

Mama became very depressed, and she developed an obsessive jealousy over my father.

One day, when I came home from school, I went down the hall to my bedroom to put my stuff on my bed. When I passed the open door to my parents' room, I saw her going through my dad's clothes that were hanging in the closet.

"I'm home." I thought the sound of my voice

Rebel Boy

would startle her, but she didn't even glance in my direction.

"The evidence. I'm looking for it."

"Evidence?"

"Your father has another woman, and I'm going to find lipstick on one of his shirts. You'll see. I know you don't believe me. Come, Matthew. I'll show you what I already found."

She beckoned to me as she walked over to her nightstand. Standing there, she pointed a shaky finger at something lying on a book beside her bedside lamp.

"See?" She turned on the lamp.

"No. What is there to see?"

Carefully, she picked something up between her thumb and forefinger and held it out so I could see it. "A hair. Blonde."

There was a look of triumph mixed with pain on her face as she stood there holding onto a tiny hair.

"That could have come from… anywhere. Papa rides a bus to and from work. There are 45 to 50 people on it."

Snatching her hand back, her gaze flashing fire, she said, "Believe what you like. I know. I have the evidence."

This went on for two years, and it got so that I

Stories from the Oasis

hated to come home. Then my mother started taking pills. They were prescribed by her doctor and were supposed to make her feel better, but she took so many that often there were times when she didn't even recognize me or my younger sister, Genevieve.

My father got tired of trying to defend himself against all her accusations, and when I was about 16, he decided he had to leave the house.

"Matthew, it's not because I don't love you or your sister. I'm leaving because I can't do this anymore. You know, with your mama."

When he walked out the door carrying a small suitcase, I swallowed hard trying to push down the lump that had formed in my throat. I was going to have to look after my mother and sister now. I would have to be the man of the house, all while going to high school.

When he left, I had no idea where he went, but my mother knew. He would call once in a while, but she wouldn't tell us where he was or let us talk to him.

With my father gone, my mother tried to kill herself. One afternoon, I came home from school and found her in the bathroom. She had cut herself, and there was blood all over. Frightened out of my mind, I ran across the street where one of my

Rebel Boy

uncles lived.

"Mama has cut herself, and she is bleeding a lot."

As he called the ambulance, I ran back home where I wrapped a towel around her arm and wrist and held it tightly there until the ambulance came and took her to the hospital. After that, I had to watch her constantly.

My father was gone a month. When he came back, things were better between my parents for a while, but it didn't last. He took my sister and me aside one day. "Your mama is very sick. Today, I'm taking her to the hospital."

The "hospital" turned out to be a government institution where mentally disturbed people were taken. My father took me and my sister to visit my mother. When we pulled up and parked outside the building, I saw there were bars on the windows. The building was very rundown, and it was surrounded by dirt — nothing green around as far as the eye could see.

Inside, we passed little cell-like rooms just barely large enough for one person, and there were padlocks on the doors. Some of the rooms were larger with small groups of people inside. These were for the less severe cases. My mother was in one of these rooms. They had medicated her so

Stories from the Oasis

much that she wasn't as bad as the people in the cells.

The place was dirty and looked like it hadn't been cleaned for months. There was litter on the floor. There were no beds, just a piece of metal that pulled out from the wall and hung suspended by a chain at each end with a very thin pad on it for a mattress and one thin blanket. As we walked along a row of cells, we could hear other inmates, and I saw Genevieve put her hands up, covering her ears to block the screams, pretending she couldn't hear.

The minute I saw my mother, she slipped silently into the shadows of the old stone building. My father, sister and I stood silently by the door and waited. As we watched, my mother slowly crept towards us. She was dirty from head to toe, and her hair was a dark mass of tangles around her face. She wore a tattered, dirty uniform. She watched us for a moment, and I saw her take a deep, steadying breath to calm herself.

Standing there, I wondered what demon had fashioned this place. She was living in hell itself, or at least man's version of it.

"Father, we have to take her out of here. How much longer can she endure this?"

With an exasperated sigh he said, "Yes. We will take her home and try again." He looked so tired.

Rebel Boy

So terribly, incredibly tired.

"Matthew," my mother said softly. "Genevieve." She gently touched my sister's sleeve. "You have come to see me."

Her desperate gaze turned to my father, and she started to cry. "I'm sorry. I'm so sorry. You have come to take me home, yes?"

Genevieve and I waited outside by the car while my father took care of my mother's release. Staring at the ground, I decided I would force myself never to think of this again. I would bury it deep inside. It was all like a horror movie.

My mother was home for almost a month, and then she started to fail. The doctor prescribed about 10 different kinds of pills and said she would have to take them for the rest of her life. When my parents went to bed at night, I stayed up to see if they were going to fight.

Curled up tightly on the couch, I would start to doze off, and suddenly my head would jerk up, and I was awake again. The hours dragged by. My legs were cramped in the tight confines of the narrow couch, and in the morning, my back and shoulders ached, and a dull pain nagged at the back of my neck. Fear hovered in our house like a heavy morning mist.

One night, a couple of hours before dawn, my

Stories from the Oasis

father came out into the living room and slumped into a chair. "You're awake. I'm sorry," he spoke into the inky darkness of the room.

"Matthew, I have tried everything. One of your aunts suggested we take your mama to church. Tomorrow is Sunday. Let's give it a try."

The next morning, we took Mama to church, and immediately, we noticed a change for the better.

"What do you think, Father?"

"I don't know what to think, but suddenly she's doing better."

We started using the church like a hospital. Every time she was feeling bad, we would take her to church, and she would get better. When we didn't take her, she got worse.

Our pastor came to the house and prayed for her, and she would be fine for a couple of days. When he didn't come, she got worse.

"We are all going to go to church," my father announced. "It's the only thing that's helping Mama."

It was amazing, but with regular church attendance, my mother got better and better. My parents even started serving the Lord in some of the ministries of the church.

At age 18, I was more into partying than going

Rebel Boy

to church. I was really rebelling. Some good friends and I — three of us — got together regularly and went out. We lived close to a very small tourist town, and we knew all the owners of the discos, clubs and casino. People got to know us, and we became "famous" in town. We drank at the clubs. The owners would give us free passes, and we would make money off of them.

At the disco, I talked to one of the owners. "Say, tomorrow night, I need 15 free passes."

He forked them over, and then I went outside the building, and all of us stood right by the front door and sold them. We needed money so we could go to the casino because we had started gambling.

In the disco, I would drink and meet girls. If we ended up having sex, that was fine with me. On Mondays, sometimes, I would see the girl I had been with the night before. Usually, I couldn't remember her, but I would get a funny feeling that made me feel like, "Do I know you?"

The drug for me was marijuana. I smoked pot, and sometimes we even sold small amounts. We knew who to go to because we had connections. Thinking I could hide this from my parents, I chewed gum and told myself, "They will never know," but my clothes reeked of it.

Stories from the Oasis

My parents tried hard to keep me on the right path and in church. My father said, "As long as you live under this roof, we will make the rules."

Whenever I was drunk, I would try to sneak into the house without them hearing me, but they always found me. One time, it was so late when I came home that the sun was starting to come up. My parents were up and getting ready for church when I tried to sneak into my room.

"Oh no, you don't!" my father growled as he collared me.

"What?"

"You're going to church with the rest of us!"

Before I knew what happened, he had me down on my bed and was pulling my clothes off. Then he dragged me into the shower and turned the cold water on full blast.

Still feeling pretty rotten, I got myself dressed, and we went to church. That particular Sunday, the pastor asked me to help him pass out some fliers. I could still smell alcohol on myself, and I was sure the people at church could, too. With my long hair and my "rebel boy" attitude, I felt self-conscious in church, but I didn't feel bad enough to stop going out drinking with the guys.

Making my way to one of the rear pews, I sat down by myself. My thoughts drifted away from

Rebel Boy

the sermon and back to when I was a little kid. When I was 6 years old, all of us in the family went to church, except my father. I don't know why he didn't go, but he let my mother, Genevieve and I go. In Sunday school, I learned about Jesus. My mother told me that when I was 6, I developed a tender love in my heart for Jesus, but I don't remember that.

We went to church regularly until we moved to Salinas. Then we stopped going.

Now, as I sat alone in that pew, I tried hard to recapture the feelings my mother said I had in my heart for Jesus when I was 6 years old, but to no avail.

Around this time, I started half-heartedly attending the church's youth events, but I didn't give up my "other life." My excuse was, "Why go to these events? We don't have enough kids in our church — just a bunch of old people. The disco has thousands of kids."

Walking around town on a Saturday, if I saw people from church, I would try to hide from them. I found myself hating people and hating church. My mother liked to play worship music in the house, but I couldn't stand it. Sneaking up behind her, I would turn it off and then disappear.

My life changed dramatically when a youth

Stories from the Oasis

group from Argentina, a team of 15-20 kids, came to town.

"Wow! This is great. What cool kids." The week they were in town, I attended their events, enjoyed their music and worship and sang right along with them. That week touched my heart in a special way, and the last night they were there, something wonderful happened.

As one of the group was talking about how awesome Jesus was and how we should be living our lives for him, something inside me stirred. It was a feeling of love and warmth that had been bottled up inside me for years, and now it was free to flow through me again. Without any awkward feelings or hesitation, I went down on my knees. "Lord, I surrender all to you." I found salvation at that meeting.

Immediately, I stopped smoking pot and drinking. It took a little bit longer for me to stop going out, but when I did, I got involved in the church.

I met Pastor Barney Huie for the first time when he came to Uruguay with about 20 other pastors on a mission trip. He had a translator who couldn't be with him all the time, so I was assigned to take him around and show him the city. We became friends. At the end of his trip, he returned to

Rebel Boy

the United States and his church in Memphis, Tennessee. About a year later, he invited me to come for a visit. I didn't have the money, so my church helped with that, and the church in Memphis bought my ticket.

It was August when I arrived, and I met many wonderful people at the church. Through my friendship with the pastor's kids, I met a man and went to work for him in his painting business.

In September, a lovely young woman named Daisy came to the church. She was from Louisiana, but she was staying in Memphis while she went to optometry school. The guy who played the keyboard went to school with her and invited her to the church.

That first Sunday when I saw her, I couldn't take my eyes off of her. She had beautiful chestnut-colored hair and cool, brown eyes. I fell in love on the spot.

The next Sunday, she came back, and I started talking with her. When I asked her out, she didn't seem very interested.

"I'm sorry, Matthew. I just don't have the time."

Telling me she was too busy didn't deter me. I kept after Daisy for a month until she finally agreed to go out to dinner with me. We started

Stories from the Oasis

dating, and she invited me to spend Christmas in Louisiana with her family. We all got along great, and I had a wonderful time.

My visa expired, and it was time for me to return to Uruguay. The night before I left, I went to her house. We sat together on a swing on the front porch. Our conversation was hesitant, and some of the long pauses were punctuated by the chirping of the crickets. It was so difficult to bring myself to say goodbye.

"Daisy, I really don't want to say goodbye to you. My heart hurts."

"It's going to be … different without you here."

As her voice started to break, I reached over and took her hand in mine. "We belong together. Do you feel it?"

"We need to pray. Ask God if this is what he wants for us."

Not able to prolong the pain of leaving her, after we prayed, I gave her a quick little kiss on the cheek and sprinted to my car. Glancing in the rearview mirror as I peeled away from the curb, I saw her standing on the porch, waving. The porch light was like a spotlight on Daisy, and that scene was etched into my memory.

We wrote each other letters and emails and talked on the phone. The time and distance started

Rebel Boy

to prove to both of us that our relationship was serious. I returned to the States a couple of times, and once, she came to Uruguay and stayed for a week. Beyond any doubt, we were in love and wanted to be married.

We started the paperwork, and at the end of the year, I came to the U.S. We got married on New Year's Eve in Louisiana.

We lived in Memphis for about six months, but by that time, Pastor Barney had left and gone to Rockwall, Texas.

"Honey, I feel that God is calling us to Rockwall."

"Matthew, I had a dream the other night that we were in Rockwall. I think we should go."

It was a leap of faith on our part as we went to Rockwall, Texas. Within a week, I had found a job painting. The idea of having my own business was growing and growing, and finally, I started a painting and remodeling business. This was another step in faith, and God was good and opened some doors. Daisy had been working as a fill-in for busy eye doctors here and there, but finally, as if by divine appointment, she interviewed and got the job of full-time optometrist for Wal-Mart.

God has blessed me so much. As soon as I stopped rebelling, I was able to hear Jesus

Stories from the Oasis

knocking at the door of my heart. When I opened that door and let him in, my life changed completely. My mother continues to be well, and she and my father are still very active in their church in Uruguay.

God led my beautiful wife and me to the Oasis Church in Rockwall. The church embraced us, and it has been great working with Pastor Barney again. Daisy and I have a home group called H2O. People come over to our house, and we go through whatever the pastor preached the previous Sunday. Another purpose for the group is to build relationships, and all of us learn so much.

My greatest life lesson has been that God can do anything! Trust him, and have faith and confidence to go wherever he leads.

Rebel Boy

"Show me your ways, O Lord,
teach me in your paths;
guide me in your truth and teach me,
for you are God my Savior,
and my hope is in you all day long.
Remember, O Lord, your great mercy and love,
for they are from of old.
Remember not the sins of my youth
and my rebellious ways;
according to your love remember me,
for you are good, O Lord."
(Psalm 25:4-7)

4
FILLED
The Story of Lynn Broeske
Written by Angela Prusia

I had to run away or I'd kill her. The thought crashed through my conscious mind for the first time in 14 years.

"You can't speak to her like that!" I yelled. My body shook with anger. "Yolanda's my friend." I'd never talked back to my mother before. My outburst surprised her and me.

"You're a sorry excuse for a daughter," she spit in my face. I could smell the alcohol. "You'll never amount to anything." I'd heard these words so often, they were my mantra. I believed them.

My mother lunged at me, punching me in the face, like always. Sometimes I wondered if my features reminded her of the mistake she'd made when she had me. At age 14 — my age now — she hadn't been ready to become a mother.

My skin tightened with the swelling. I'd lie about the bruise, just like I had so many times before. The pain seared my flesh, but it was nothing compared to watching Yolanda suffer.

She cowered in the corner, her eyes round saucers of fear. No one had ever spent the night with me before, and now, Yolanda knew my secret of the abuse I'd endured for years. I lost count of my mother's boyfriends, just like the number of cities we'd lived in. The one time I'd been put in foster care, we were transients in Arkansas. The judge

Stories from the Oasis

dismissed the case, and I was back with my mother. We hit the road for Texas. I knew if I said anything in the courtroom, life would be worse at home.

My mother screamed more obscenities before she slumped to the floor. I was used to the mood swings. If she wasn't drunk, she was strung out on some type of drug — prescription or not. Addiction was an understatement. My mother was a wreck.

"I can't stay," Yolanda whispered. "I'm sorry." Her hands trembled as she reached for the phone. Her father was there in minutes.

I stared at my mother, now sobbing uncontrollably. If only my father would rescue me, but he'd left before my first birthday.

"I'll run to the store and get some Tylenol," I told my mother. She was through controlling my life. I walked out the door and never came back.

***

I huddled under a bridge a few blocks from our apartment, but my t-shirt and jeans offered little warmth. Dirt dug into my backside. I was alone in the world — a frightened kid with no money, no food and no plan, other than escape. Tears filled

Filled

my eyes as memories assaulted me.

"Stop, Mama, stop!" I yelled, as she beat me with an electrical cord. I grabbed the towel and tried to protect my body. Red stripes appeared on my flesh. I was still wet from the shower.

I rocked back and forth, trying to block out the nightmares I didn't want to relive, but they wouldn't stop. I remembered staring at the clock for hours one summer day as I sat in a hot car. I could see Mama through the tattered drapes. I was only 7, but I knew what she was doing. I could see her shooting up drugs with the other addicts. Her arms were pockmarked with scars.

"Come on, Mama," I pleaded, though she couldn't hear me. "Can't we go home?" I wanted to play with my doll. My stomach hurt from hunger.

Hours later, my clothes wet with sweat, Mama got into our car and slammed the door. She screamed at someone who stood in the doorway of the house and then drove straight to the hospital. No one took me from my hell. The system failed again. Mama was still messed up. I was still under her care, an easy target for her every rampage.

"Lynn?" a voice called out. "Is that you?" It was Jana, one of my friends from the apartment complex. She was with a half dozen kids, but they were too busy drinking to notice me. The bridge was a

Stories from the Oasis

favorite hangout.

"What's wrong?" Jana sat beside me. The gentleness in her voice unleashed emotions I wanted to hide.

When I told her what happened, Jana took me to her place. Her parents didn't ask questions. We lived in a rough section of Dallas; dysfunction was the norm. For the next five months, I hid from my mother. My friends pitched in to bring me clothes and food, and they even did my laundry.

I refused to go outside. I was sure my mother would find me.

"Come on," Jana's boyfriend, John, said one night. "Let's go hang out at my house. Have some fun."

I shook my head.

"You gonna stay inside forever?"

I didn't fight when John and his friend, James, pulled me toward the door.

They were right. A girl can only stay inside for so long. I was about to go crazy. Besides, John was 19, and James was 23. They could drive.

Freedom was nice, even if we only hung out at a different house.

"Yeehaw!" John shouted when we hit the road to go back to Jana's place. I was sandwiched between the two guys, the wind on my face. I wanted

Filled

to raise my hands in the air and scream until my throat hurt. I was a prisoner set free.

For all of five minutes. When I heard the siren, my heart sank. The flashing lights signaled for us to pull over.

"You know you got a busted taillight?" the officer said.

I shrunk in my seat, trying to make myself invisible. It didn't work. My mother had filed a missing person's report. The police tried to reach her, but she wasn't home. I was taken to my grandmother.

I barricaded myself in the room when my mother finally showed up. I heard her arguing with my grandmother.

"Is she here?" my mother barked.

"Lynn's staying this time." I could hear the resolve in my grandmother's voice.

"No, she's not!" my mother screamed.

"Yes, I am," I whispered from behind the safety of the door.

"I've been worried sick."

"Don't lie," I hissed.

My grandmother said something, but she wasn't loud like my mother.

"Lynn's been gone for almost half a year — just hanging out with her friends — and all the while, I

Stories from the Oasis

think one of the lowlifes I know has taken her." The confession was laced with anger. "Lynn's coming home. She needs to learn a thing or two about respect."

My grandmother's voice rose, and I knew it was for my benefit. "Lynn wants to live with me."

Profanity spewed from my mother's mouth.

"She's tired of moving around all the time." My grandmother's voice caught. "Has the child ever gone to a school more than one year?"

"No," I whispered. How many friends had I made, only to have to say goodbye?

"So, it's my fault my photography takes me all over?"

My grandmother's voice softened. "Let Lynn stay here. She needs stability."

In the past, my mother would threaten my grandmother when she didn't get her way. "Give me money, or you won't ever see your granddaughter again," Mama would say. But here I was, changing the game. Now, the pawn and the queen mother declared checkmate.

My mother and I spoke all of five minutes the entire next year, and then she was jailed for running drugs. When she was released, she jumped parole and went to California. I wasn't surprised when my mother was found dead in an alcove be-

Filled

tween two buildings. A passerby had called the police when he noticed her body hadn't moved in two days. The coroner's report didn't list the cause of death.

***

I dug the knife deep into my flesh until the pain made me cry out.

"You're a loser," I told myself. The mirror reflected my hollow eyes. "You'll never amount to anything."

I lifted the knife and watched blood drip off the silver blade. Drip. Drip. Drip. A red river ran across the scars that crisscrossed my flesh. Long-sleeve shirts hid my secret.

A knock on my door startled me. I shoved the knife under my bed. "Who is it?"

My grandmother twisted the knob on the door. "Can I come in?" When I nodded, she sat on my bed.

"You don't have to sneak food out of the refrigerator, Lynn," she said. "You can eat whatever you want, whenever you want."

I lowered my eyes. My mother always used food as a weapon. There were always restrictions — if she let me eat at all.

Stories from the Oasis

My grandmother got up. "Don't forget. This is your home now." She shut the door behind her.

So why did I feel so empty inside? Would I ever feel like I was at home?

***

"I'm pregnant," I told my boyfriend.

"So, get an abortion."

"I can't."

"Whatever," he shrugged. "Do what you want. It's your life. I'm not taking care of any kid."

Any kid? What happened to his promises nine months ago? I caressed my stomach and imagined the baby growing inside me. My boyfriend made the decision sound so easy, so why couldn't I agree?

I rode the fence for the first trimester. My grandparents weren't happy, especially since I still had two years of school left, but they didn't kick me out of their home.

"I know this couple," my best friend said one day. "Dirk's an electrician, and Lisa's a teacher. She just delivered stillborn twins."

My heart ached for this woman I didn't even know. Had she held the twins, their tiny bodies lifeless? The very word *stillborn* unnerved me.

FILLED

"Anyway," my friend continued, "I guess Lisa can't have kids now, and she wants to adopt."

When I met Lisa at my friend's Halloween party, something stirred within me when I saw the compassion in her green eyes. We talked for a long time, and I could tell her wound was still fresh — just like my own. I felt like I could tell her anything, and she would understand.

"Do you really want to adopt my baby?" I asked Lisa before I left the party.

"More than anything." Her smile reached into my heart. The people at the adoption agencies said I would know my baby's parents when I met them. They were right. I knew Lisa was the one.

"You need to meet my husband," Lisa said. "I know this great Italian restaurant where you can get to know him."

A few weeks later, I wiped the sweat from my hands as I looked across the table at Dirk. His happy-go-lucky manner immediately relaxed my fears.

"How're you feeling?" Lisa asked.

"Okay," I said. My own insecurities were magnified by my changing body.

I could tell Dirk was getting uncomfortable. The smile disappeared from his face. "How do we know you won't change your mind?"

Stories from the Oasis

"Dirk," Lisa put her hand against his arm. "We talked about this. We can trust Lynn."

"I won't let my heart get broken again," Dirk said to his wife. "What if she decides to take the baby from us?"

"I won't," I promised. How could I make him understand? Emotion lodged in my throat. I refused to make my mother's mistake. If only she'd given me up for adoption.

Lisa squeezed her husband's arm. With her other hand, she reached out to me, so that the three of us formed a circle. "We can't know the future." Lisa looked from Dirk to me to my stomach. "But we have to trust each other." Her eyes filled with tears. "For the baby. Our baby."

***

"Breathe," Lisa coached me.

"I am," I said through clenched teeth.

"Just like the nurse showed you." Lisa was patient, just like she'd been at every doctor's appointment and every session of Lamaze.

"I can't do this again." I'd been to the hospital twice now, only to be sent home when nothing happened.

Lisa patted my hand. "This baby's gonna come.

Filled

He can't hang out there forever." She pointed to my bulging belly, and we both laughed.

"Do you think I hurt him when I tripped?" I asked. The dark clouds outside my hospital window didn't help my hormone-charged emotions.

"It could've happened to anyone." Lisa waved off my fears, and I wondered what fears she held as she remembered looking into the face of not one dead child, but two.

"But I felt my stomach jolt."

"Honey," Lisa said as she looked into my eyes, "you tripped on the curb. The baby's fine. You're going to do great."

The nurses checked me regularly throughout the day. Just when I thought the doctor would send me home again, my contractions came on strong.

"I think I'm having a baby," I squeaked.

A grin lit up Lisa's face.

"It's time to push," the doctor said.

The swing of the minute hand was interrupted with my cries of pain. At 6:26 p.m., another cry pierced the delivery room.

"He's beautiful," Lisa said, as the nurse held him to my face. I stared at his small body. 10 perfect toes. A head of dark hair. Tiny eyes that searched my face.

"Hey, little guy," I whispered. "We've been

Stories from the Oasis

waiting to meet you."

Lisa looked at me. I knew she was dying to hold her son.

"I want you to meet someone." I touched his cheek.

Lisa gulped when I handed him to her.

"Meet your mama," I said. "She already loves you more than you know."

Tears trickled down Lisa's face.

"Thank you," Lisa whispered to me. She kissed her baby, and a peace I couldn't explain filled me.

***

I broke up with my boyfriend after my son was born. I graduated and got a job at a lumber company, where I met my husband, Josh. He took me to dinner and dancing, and I fell in love. We decided to get married. Soon after, we found out I was pregnant with our son, Tyler.

Like most couples, our early years were busy with work and family. Josh and I worked opposite shifts, but we were excited with the purchase of our first home and cars.

When Josh decided to start a lawn business, the extra hours from two jobs put a real strain on our marriage. Life seemed weighted by one stress after

Filled

another. I was headstrong, but Josh had his issues, too. The death of his grandfather, a father figure since his parents' divorce, left a void in his life. Still, when Josh filed for divorce after our son, Colton, was born, I was floored.

"Give me one reason why I should stay?" Josh yelled.

"I could give you 100, not the least of which are the two kids sleeping down the hall," I screamed back. "We're not quitters. We've been through so much already. We don't give up."

Josh slammed the door behind him, ripping my heart to pieces.

I met with the lawyer a few weeks later to sign the papers. The dull ache growing inside me intensified. My marriage was over, and I couldn't do anything to stop it.

"You're not going to believe this," she said.

I stared at the lawyer, confused. "What?"

"Your husband wants to reconcile."

Was this some kind of cruel joke? Now was not the time to play with my emotions.

"I'm serious," the lawyer said. "Josh says he's had a change of heart. The two of you are going to make this work. He's been the child of divorce, and he can't do this to your kids."

I was dumbfounded. *Change of heart?* Four

Stories from the Oasis

years later, I learned who changed Josh's heart. His name was Jesus.

***

"Come to church with us," Sharon said. Josh coached our boys' baseball team. "Oasis Church is small, just like family."

"I don't know," I hesitated. Josh's grandfather was a preacher, and every time I went to church, I cried. I asked Josh about my tears, but he pushed my questions aside. Later he told me he wasn't ready to repent. Unlike me, he'd been raised in church and strayed. Josh wasn't going to play church. If he was going on Sunday, his life Monday through Saturday would have to change.

"We're having this contest to grow our church." Sharon and her husband, Shane, explained more details, but I only half listened. I had a lot of excuses. Finally, I agreed to take our family to church on the last Sunday of the contest.

The worship music started, and I could feel the familiar tears well up in my eyes. Before long, I was sobbing. *What's wrong with me?* I wondered. When Pastor Barney preached, I felt like he had read my mail. The sermon was written for me.

We woke up late the next Sunday, and I was

FILLED

secretly glad. I wouldn't have to lie to Sharon when she asked about church. Colton wouldn't hear our excuses. "We gotta go!" He jumped on our bed until we got up and got ready.

During the altar call, Josh practically ran up front. The Holy Spirit had convicted him, and he knew it was time to live for God. My own legs were dead weight. I couldn't walk up to the altar alone, but I knew we'd found our church home.

Sundays and Wednesdays weren't enough. We were starving children presented with a feast. On Saturday nights, we found friendship and accountability when we joined a *How 2 Overcome* (H2O) group. On a Wednesday night service in Pastor's home, I was crying again. "I can't do this on my own, God." His wife, Cindy, had prayed with me the week before.

Pastor's voice cut through my tears. "Let's gather around Lynn," he said. Whispered prayers rose around me. That night, I asked Jesus into my heart. Josh, Tyler and I were baptized soon after that.

Sometimes I feel so ignorant of God's word. I look at all the wasted years in my life, and I think I should be at a certain level in my faith because of my age. But God is so good. He has sped our growth like he says he will in Joel: "I will repay you

Stories from the Oasis

for the years the locusts have eaten ... You will have plenty to eat, until you are full, and you will praise the name of the Lord your God, who has worked wonders for you; never again will my people be shamed. Then you will know ... that I am the Lord your God, and that there is no other."

***

When I think about all God has done in my life, I can hardly believe what I see. I'm in the same body, and yet everything is different. I understand what Jesus meant when he answered Nicodemus: "I tell you the truth, no one can enter the kingdom of God unless he is born of water and the Spirit ... flesh gives birth to flesh, but the Spirit gives birth to spirit ... you must be born again."

Jesus is all the difference in my life. I quit smoking after 15 years and stopped cursing. Two years of therapy helped me deal with my issues of abuse, but my anger left the day I forgave my mother. Now I'm so much calmer. Josh quit drinking, and our marriage is stronger than it's ever been. Even Tyler and Colton have changed. And since we've started tithing, we have more money than we've ever had — even when we took a leap of faith with Josh's lawn business and decided I

FILLED

should stay home with the boys. Lisa and I remain in touch, so I even get to see my firstborn. I don't want to force anything in our relationship, but I pray he meets Jesus, too.

People blame God for a lot, but I don't. Not only do I see God's hand in my life, I see my own capacity to sin, and I have a deep appreciation for God's grace. I've been touched by my Maker, and I know he's real.

Now as I look to my future, I'm excited to see where God will lead me. I rest on his promise in Jeremiah: "'For I know the plans I have for you,' declares the Lord, 'plans to prosper you and not to harm you, plans to give you hope and a future.'" Josh's heart beats for young people, kids desperate for strong male role models. When teenagers see this massive guy worship God, I know they will be moved like I am. God is casting his vision in my husband toward youth ministry, and I want to support him. I pray that I can help young girls facing similar battles to mine. Boyfriends won't fill the emptiness inside. Only God can. He alone has given me hope. I'm finally home. Jesus filled me.

5
THE SCAR REMOVED
The Story of Julia
Written by Amanda Lawrence

I looked behind me, hearing the footsteps of my pursuer. My legs screamed in pain, as my feet slapped against the sidewalk. My heart raced. The sun beat down on me, and I felt sweat trickle down my temple. I knew he would hurt me. *I must find a place to hide. I don't know what he is going to do, but he will hurt me,* I thought. My chest ached as I breathed in the humid air surrounding me, dropping like a wet blanket over my shoulders. I dodged around a couple in front of me and slipped into a clothing store. Round racks of women's and men's clothing surrounded me. No one else was in sight. No customers. No salespeople. I moved away from the glass door towards the back of the store, where there was a line of doors leading to dressing rooms. I glanced behind me as I weaved my way through racks of women's pants and blouses. Halfway through the store, the bell jingled against the glass door. Without looking, I dropped down, crawling under a rack of pants. I tried to control my breathing. *Quiet. Deep, silent breaths or he'll hear me. He'll find me,* I commanded to myself. His footsteps thudded on the thin carpet, and I heard a rack spinning as he knocked against it. Metal scraped against metal as he moved clothes aside to look beneath the rack. He moved onto the next. And the next. And the next. My breathing

Stories from the Oasis

did not slow down. My stomach turned over, and I felt nauseous. I could hear him getting closer. His footsteps were louder. He pushed aside the clothes in the rack next to me. *He's gonna find me. He's gonna hurt me.*

    I wake up. A cold sweat runs over me, and I shiver. I look over at the clock and see that my husband's alarm will go off in three minutes. *Not again. I'm so tired of these nightmares. Why do I continue to have them? They started when I was 9, and 21 years is too long to have the same dream,* I think. Fear surrounds me. The shrill beep of the alarm echoes in the quiet, dark room. My husband rolls over and shuts off the alarm. Within five minutes, he is gone. I didn't want to tell him that I had my nightmare again, and I was afraid to go back to sleep. I start to sing. *The enemy has been defeated. And death couldn't hold you down. I'm gonna lift my voice in victory. I'm gonna make your praises loud.* I fall asleep.

**

    My parents separated when I was 5. I had a close relationship with my dad, even though I don't remember too much about him. I only remember my feel-good memories of him. He took

The Scar Removed

me and my older brother, Jacob, to the park to play on the playground or to the gas station for candy. However, he was an alcoholic and physically abusive. One incident of his rage fell on Jacob when he was 7 and I was 5.

"Dad, can I go play across the street with Tony?" Jacob asked my dad, who was lounging in his easy chair, a beer in his hand.

He jumped from the chair, yelling. "You stay home! I don't want you going anywhere!" He grabbed Jacob around the neck and threw him into the living room wall of our trailer house.

My brother moaned and started to cry. He slid to the floor. Above him, there was an imprint of his body on the wall. Soon after, my parents were divorced.

I felt the loss of my dad's love. The last time I saw my dad, I was 6, but I talked to him on the phone when I was 9. He and his new wife, Gwen, wanted Jacob, my younger brother, Joey, and me to come from Texas to visit them in Minnesota. Joey and I left the decision to visit up to Jacob. Because he felt that it wasn't a good thing, I told Dad that we wouldn't be coming.

"Your mother has poisoned you against me, hasn't she?" he asked.

"No, Dad, Mom has nothing to do with our

Stories from the Oasis

decision not to come visit," I told him.

Gwen called me some profane names. That was the last time we ever heard from him. I felt guilty and that it was my fault that my brothers and I never heard from him again.

My mother remarried when I was 7. One day, not long after they were married, her husband, Arthur, took my brothers to school and made me stay home. Mom was working, and he took me into their bedroom. I've blocked the details of what happened that day, but I'm aware that I learned about the male physique. Hours later, after lunch, we went to the store. I saw some puppies for sale, and Arthur bought me two, one female and one male. I named them Bonnie and Clyde. *I wonder if male doggie's bodies act the same way as male body parts act,* I thought to myself. He sexually abused me until I was 8, making it all a "game." I never told Mom that he abused me, but she still left him after only a year of marriage. He dropped us off at my mom's older sister's house with just the clothes on our back.

We lived with that aunt for a time, then my mom met another man, and we moved in with him. That relationship did not last long, and soon we moved into an apartment of our own. Mom worked three jobs to pay for the rent, so we didn't

The Scar Removed

see a lot of her. We were independent and learned to take care of ourselves. She had a difficult time keeping an eye on us, as well as making sure we had enough money to keep the roof over our heads. When I was 9, my mom's younger sister, Tia, and her husband, Ahab, moved to a town closer to us. Since Mom was working so many hours, she felt that my brothers and I should live with them for the summer.

Their two-bedroom apartment was completely furnished, except for the spare room which they used for storage. My brothers and I had to sleep in the living room on the pullout couch, unless we were privileged to sleep in their bed. I was the only one privileged. I felt secure knowing that Aunt Tia would be there with me. Little did I realize that she would be a willing, active participant in my uncle's molestation of me. Uncle Ahab took naked pictures of me and Aunt Tia together in different poses. He also introduced me to porn. *I need to make men happy in order to keep them around. I'll do whatever they ask of me. What they are doing to me isn't wrong. It's all in fun. It's natural. These things happen.* I told myself all of these things, believing them.

My brothers and I had complete run of the apartment complex and access to the pool. Occa-

123

Stories from the Oasis

sionally, my aunt would drop us off at the movie theater. Sometimes my aunt would take Jacob and Joey somewhere, leaving me alone with Uncle Ahab.

I didn't realize that I was doing something wrong. Uncle Ahab was a truck driver and needed to take a shipment to Colorado, so I went on a two-day trip with him. When we returned, my uncle had to go out again.

Aunt Tia confronted me while I was unpacking. "What did you do while you were gone? Did you spend all of your time in the hotel room? You little slut! Do you think you're special, trying to steal my husband?" she raged at me.

Tears welled in my eyes. "What? I've only done what I've been told to do. I was only trying to make him happy."

"I'm all he should need to make him happy. Do you honestly believe that what you're doing is just a game? It's not. You're ruining my life. My husband comes home and then leaves again. All because of you. Do you think that you're all he needs now? I'm his wife, and you're just his little whore for the summer," she seethed.

Horrified, I cried out, "I'm sorry! I didn't know. Why didn't you stop it? Why did you let it happen? I didn't know it was wrong!" I shivered,

The Scar Removed

even though the room was stuffy because the air-conditioner wasn't working.

"Get out of my sight!" she ranted. "Before I do something I'll regret."

I ran from the living room and down to the pool. Jacob waved from the deep end, and I barely lifted my hand back in a semblance of a wave. I dropped onto a chaise lounge and closed my eyes. Guilt weighed on my shoulders, and I felt dirty. No amount of bathing would take this dirt away.

Jacob swam to the side of the pool. "You okay?" he asked.

"Yeah," I told him. "Aunt Tia just yelled at me. She's upset about Uncle Ahab leaving again so soon and took it out on me. I'll be okay."

"Alright, just checking." He pushed away from the side of the pool.

I didn't tell him what transpired because I was afraid that he would get in Uncle Ahab's face and demand to know what was going on. After the summer was over and I returned home, I didn't tell anyone about what had happened.

Uncle Ahab passed away when he was in his mid-40s, less than a year after our summer spent with him. I was 10 when Aunt Tia moved into our two-bedroom apartment with us. My brothers and I shared a bedroom, which she took over and

Stories from the Oasis

moved into. One day, I had to go into the room to search for something. All of her stuff, and some of my uncle's stuff, covered the floor like a blanket. It was everywhere. I found one of the naked pictures of Aunt Tia and me, and I felt this shame fall over me because of what I had done. I realized that what they had done to me that summer was not something a child should go through. I destroyed that picture, but I don't know what happened to the rest of the pictures. I haven't spoken to Aunt Tia since she moved out.

 I spent time with my brothers and their friends, but did not have any girlfriends. School came easy to me, and it was a safe haven. When I wasn't at school, I kept to myself at home.

 "Are you going to play soccer this year?" a friend asked me after my summer spent with my aunt and uncle.

 "Uh, I don't think I'm going to play this year," I told her, ducking my head.

 "Why not? You've always played in the past. And you're really good. The team can really use you," she said.

 "I just don't have time. I spend a lot of time with my brothers. I've been going on ski trips with them and have been so busy," I lied to her, because all I did was stay at home. I just wanted to seclude

The Scar Removed

myself at home. The end of my summer with my aunt and uncle was also the end to my extracurricular activities. *There's something wrong with me. People don't want to know me or see the real me. I'm not someone that people want to be around,* I thought. I lived a lie about my life because there was nothing to my life.

I did have exposure to church growing up. Mom was always trying to get us to go. From the time I was 8, she would have the church bus pick us up. I felt like I was hiding from God.

Sometimes when the bus would come for us, we would hide in the apartment and not answer the door like we weren't home so the bus would go on without us. When I was 12, my mom remarried. Her third husband's mother was a solid Christian, and she took me and my brothers to church with her.

I'm so uncomfortable here, I thought one Sunday in church. *I wish I didn't have to keep coming. I have so much shame over what I did. God couldn't love me. I'm not a good person. I'll find some way to get out of coming. I hate being here all the time. I won't talk to anyone. They may try to get too close to me and find out I'm not someone they want to know.*

I didn't have many relationships anyhow. I

Stories from the Oasis

basically kept to myself and lived in the fantasy world of my life. I had one girlfriend, Wendy, in high school that I would go to movies and games with, but I didn't really have a close friendship with her. My junior year, my boyfriend, Phil, was on the baseball team. I put all of my energy into him.

"Want to go to a movie this afternoon?" Wendy asked one Wednesday, standing next to my locker after school.

"No. I'm going to watch Phil practice," I responded.

"What about Friday night?" she asked.

"Can't. Phil has a game. You know I don't miss one. Maybe some other time. I gotta go," I told her, rushing down the hall towards the exit leading to the baseball field.

That night, after Phil had taken me to the drive-in for a burger, we parked down the street from my house. "I love you, baby," he told me, moving his hand up under my shirt.

I kissed him and let his hand roam. We had already had sex, so he wasn't doing anything I wasn't willing to do. *Sex between two willing parties is okay,* I told myself. After he was done, he took me home. Weeks later, when he tried to force me to do some things that my uncle had made me do, I

The Scar Removed

realized that he had his own issues he needed to take care of, so I broke up with him.

I didn't date my senior year. The only guys who asked me out were black, and my family did not want me to date anyone from a different race. I lived in a small town, so everyone pretty much knew me. I was pretty and had developed early, so I was discouraged when no one else asked me out. I found out later that my bully brothers had put the word out that if anyone hurt me, then they would be in trouble.

Then I met Michael. I was going to a nearby junior college, and I had to share a car with Mom. She was working at a local grocery store, and when I picked her up at work one day, I saw him behind the deli counter. Two months later, I had my own car. Wendy and I had similar class schedules at the college, so during our hour break, we would go to the store's salad bar for our meal.

"He's really cute. Has he asked you out yet?" she asked me.

"Not yet, but I hope he will soon," I told her, smiling at him when he glanced our way. I walked to the deli counter.

"Hi," he said.

"Hi."

"What can I do for you? Can I get you

Stories from the Oasis

something?" he asked.

"Hmm, yeah. I think I'll have the smallest container of fruit salad and chicken Caesar salad," I said. I watched as he dished up the salads, priced them and handed them over to me. After paying for them and sitting down with Wendy to eat, I continued to look his way and smiled whenever I caught his eye.

After two months of chatting and smiling, during which the holidays had passed us by, he finally asked me out. After just a few months of dating, he started to ask me to marry him. Once again, I stopped doing things with my friend, Wendy, and my life revolved around him. I lived in a fantasy world while I dated Michael. I was wearing rose-colored glasses. A year later, we married in a semi-formal wedding.

The sexual part of our marriage was great, but we were basically living separate lives. We would occasionally do things together, but I lived in my fantasy world of romance novels, and Michael watched television. We only went to church three times in 10 years, and it was only for a christening or family function. Since I grew up thinking porn was okay, my husband and I introduced it into our marriage. The only contact we had was when we had sex, and I believed that as long as I kept him

The Scar Removed

happy in our marriage bed, then everything would be okay. However, I didn't enjoy sex. I was living in my romance novel fantasy world where the men were heroes, not fallible. When I had sex with Michael, I wasn't even having sex with him but one of the characters from my novels.

We had financial problems, but we didn't fight or have any conflict between us. Then again, we had no connection to each other. After five years of marriage, we separated.

He started to spend a lot of time on the computer, shutting the door to the study. One day, after coming home from work, our dog kept sniffing him, a trait he didn't tend to do unless one of us had been around another dog or animal. I knew that he had been somewhere besides work.

When I was let off work early on the Friday before Memorial Day, I went home to look on the computer to see what he had been hiding and why he was on it all the time. He had been communicating with another woman, communicating in a way he should have been doing with me. He was supposed to meet her that weekend, until he found out that I had Memorial Day off. They cancelled their plans together. He came home to find me snooping.

"What do you think you're doing?" he asked.

Stories from the Oasis

"I wanted to see what kept you in here all the time," I told him.

"You don't trust me!" he said, pointing to me at the computer with his e-mail open. "You never talk to me. We've even stopped having sex. What did you expect?"

"I don't know. Not this."

"Not that it matters, but we haven't had sex yet. I can talk to her, and she listens. She's there for me like you haven't been. Our marriage is over. I can't do this anymore," he told me, storming out of the house.

I packed my bags and went home to my mom. During our separation of a year, Michael and I dated. We filed bankruptcy to get out of our financial debt. We got back together, but we just entered the same cycle we found ourselves in before the separation. We started out like we did right out of high school. Nothing was resolved, and we didn't discuss our issues. The only change was our financial issues. We moved into a rental for a year before we decided that it was time to own our own home.

We found a home in Royse City. Our final two choices were in two separate sections of town, but both houses had the same developer. We picked the location we did because of the friendly people.

The Scar Removed

The first neighbors we met were Ami and her children. They lived a couple of houses down. Over the next two years, Ami's husband kept inviting Michael to come to church. Finally, we decided to go.

When I walked into Oasis Church, I felt comfortable for the first time ever in a church. God's love radiated from them, and it was like walking into a room and having everyone's arms wrap around me in love. As a child, I had said the words needed to ask Jesus to save me, but they meant nothing to me at that time. Our first time at Oasis, the revelation that God loved us came to Michael and me. We never realized that before. There was a call for anyone who wished to ask Jesus into their heart and life to come forward. We both went. It was truly the first time that we accepted Christ's love and forgiveness into our lives.

I had always missed out on a father's love, and I knew that my God — my Father — loved me. He loved me when my stepfather hurt me. He loved me when my uncle and aunt molested me. He loved me when I hid in the house from him. He loved me when I had sex with my boyfriend in high school. He loved me when Michael and I had marital problems. He loved me the entire time!

I changed so much, as did Michael, that our

Stories from the Oasis

family thought we had joined a cult. It was so unusual for us to be involved, and we were at church whenever we could be there. My grandmother, a strong, Bible-believing Christian, called me and asked about the church we were going to. She wanted to make sure that we hadn't, in fact, joined a cult. I told her about the pastor's history to alleviate any fears she had. Since the first time at Oasis, I know God was working on me. The love and acceptance that I felt from the members there were very important to me. I repented of my sins on that first day, but that didn't heal me. The scarring was still there. The hurts were still there. We started to go to life groups and became involved with other couples in the church.

One Wednesday night after a meeting, Peter approached me and said, "I don't know if this will mean anything to you, but one day, you will be able to look back and not see the scar." I was amazed that though he did not know anything about my past, he was exactly right about my need for healing of those old wounds.

There was a new believer's class that Michael and I wanted to take, but because of a time conflict, we were unable to go. However, the church changed the class to Saturday nights, and we were able to attend. Peter taught this class, and we went

The Scar Removed

through a workbook on God's testimony and what God will do for you.

At the end of all of this, we had to give our testimony to the rest of the group. I felt close to and safe enough with the 12 people in the class that I could tell them what happened to me as a child. I had to write my testimony down because I knew that I wouldn't be able to get through it otherwise. I had to read it.

"It was good you wrote it down. Because you did that, something good will happen to you," Peter told me after class. "It was worth you taking the time to do that."

God continued to bring revelations to me. What happened to me wasn't my fault. I am worth something.

One Sunday morning, a woman prayed with me and told me, "You have worth. If you ask, God will show you what you should do with your thoughts and with your hands and give you what you are supposed to say."

I've always felt self-conscious about what I said for fear of sounding stupid or going out and doing things because I didn't feel I was worthy. I now have relationships with women, inside and outside of church activities. I communicate with my husband. God has given me a confidence in myself and in my abilities. I know he will take care of everything.

I still struggled with getting past the hurt. Someone told me, "You need to go back and think about the things that happened to you and feel the pain to try to get past them. You need to think about what Jesus went through for us. Think about all the pain he suffered so we wouldn't have to carry our hurts and pain from our past."

I re-experienced all the things I had been going through, and I felt a release of it. Three days later, I prayed in our small group, even though I feared praying out loud because I thought I would sound stupid. I thanked God for changing us and continuing to make us into vessels for his glory. Peter told me of a vision he saw while I was praying. He saw a ball rolling up and down my body, removing the scar. The pain was gone. I felt no shame. I felt no rejection. I felt worthy. I felt like I had something to give.

***

I looked behind me, hearing the footsteps of my pursuer. Someone is with me, and I'm holding his hand. There are tunnels in the ground all around me, and I see a man. I know it is Satan. I

The Scar Removed

run through a tunnel and hear Satan in another tunnel, so I return to ground level, holding tightly to someone's hand. He is with me every step as I try to escape Satan. I don't know how Satan moved from his tunnel to the ground level, but I see him in the distance. I stopped running. I yelled, "Satan, be gone!" Satan turned and ran.

I wake up to the alarm. My nightmare has never come back.

6
Outside Prison Walls
The Story of Shane Broeske
Written by Karen Koczwara

"One more line, man." My buddy grabbed the mirror and scraped the white powder into a neat little line with his razor. "This is my last one for the night." His bloodshot eyes suggested he hadn't slept in days.

"Whatever." I leaned back on the tattered sofa and raked my hands through my greasy, matted hair. It had been almost a week since I'd washed it, but I didn't much care. Mounting piles of laundry, beer cans and take-out boxes littered the floor. I didn't much care about that, either.

My buddy took a hit of meth and slid the mirror back toward me. Glancing down, I caught sight of my face and winced. Haunting dark circles under my eyes, scabs and sores dotting my sallow face, yellowed teeth that had seen better days. I pushed the mirror away and closed my eyes. Suddenly, three days' worth of nonstop energy had spiraled into exhaustion.

"You crashin' on me, man?" My buddy kicked his feet up on the coffee table and flicked on the TV.

I willed my eyes to open, but the simple motion seemed too difficult. Sweat poured down my back, clinging to my ratty t-shirt. Time, I realized, had become irrelevant. It could have been 10 a.m. or 10 p.m.; it was all the same to me.

Stories from the Oasis

I curled up into a ball and listened as a comedian droned on about traffic or something stupid on the TV. My life had been reduced to snorting meth in the confines of my darkened living room. Outside these four walls, the sun shone, people laughed and life went on. Meanwhile, I remained a prisoner inside my own home, the result of a choice I feared was too late to reverse.

***

I was raised by two loving parents who practiced good old-fashioned morals. My two brothers and two sisters were several years older than me, which made me a "daddy's boy" growing up. I had one younger sister close to my age, which I fought with often.

For the most part, we were the typical all-American family. I was born and raised in Rockwall, Texas, a town of 10,000 people, which provided ample opportunity for hunting, fishing and country living. My father made a decent income, thrusting us into the middle-class category growing up. My parents squabbled as most parents do from time to time, but for the most part, my childhood was idyllic.

"Shane! You comin' down? We're all ready for

Outside Prison Walls

church. Come on!" my mother's voice trilled up the stairs.

I poked my head out of my bedroom. "I'm not gonna go this morning, Mom. I'm gonna go help Dad at work. Okay?"

I heard my mother's exasperated sigh from below. "All right, but next week, I want you in that pew. Understand?"

I closed my bedroom door and flung myself back on my bed, trying to catch a few more winks of sleep. It wasn't that I disliked church. I just didn't find it terribly interesting. My father, an independent contractor, often needed help with his remodels, and I conveniently decided to give him a hand on Sunday mornings. Once in a while, I drug my heels to church to appease my mother. I liked hearing about God, and the songs we sang were kind of fun. I even got baptized at the age of 12. But the truth was there were so many more interesting things for a young boy to do on a sunny weekend morning than go to church.

Baseball was my first love. When I turned 12 years old, I got my hands on a wonderful leather mitt and a heavy wooden bat and began playing every chance I got. I loved the sound of the ball meeting the bat — a satisfying "pop" as it launched into the air. It seemed I had found my niche.

Stories from the Oasis

A rather introverted kid, I didn't have many friends in grade school. This didn't bother me much, until I got to junior high school. Suddenly, being popular seemed extremely important. I made it my goal to do everything in my power to become popular, no matter the cost. This meant making friends with the kids at the top, squeezing into their inner circle and getting invited to the best parties in town. Not an easy task for a shy kid, but I was determined to shed my quiet nature in exchange for a place at the top.

When I was 14 years old, I went over to my neighbor's house for the night. I hadn't been there more than a couple hours when he pulled a joint out of his dresser drawer. "Ever tried one?" he asked coolly, lighting the end.

I shrugged. "Nah." I knew kids who smoked pot, but I hadn't ventured that far yet. Not wanting to look ignorant, however, I grabbed the joint from my buddy's fingers and took a drag. The smoke stung the back of my lungs, but I suppressed a cough. No need to make a big deal here. It was just pot. "Not bad," I lied, handing the joint back.

"Wait till the buzz kicks in," he said, grinning. "You'll be flyin' high."

I laughed. "Right on." I had a feeling this wouldn't be the last joint I'd touch.

Outside Prison Walls

Ninth grade rolled around, and I discovered the opposite sex. Suddenly, nothing mattered more than having a pretty girl on my arm. I felt like a million bucks when a cute, blond cheerleader glanced my way and smiled. If I could keep up with the dating scene, I'd be more popular than ever.

One evening, I went over to my friend's house to spend the night. When nighttime rolled around and his parents had long gone to bed, we fished a bottle of Bacardi out of his duffel bag. "Anyone up for a little fun?" he asked, grinning mischievously.

My heart skipped a beat as my eyes fell onto the bottle of rum in his hands. "Where'd you get that?" I whispered, impressed.

"Ah, my parents got a big stash. They won't miss it. Here." He popped the top open and took a swig. A satisfied "ahh" escaped his lips. "Have some, Shane."

I obliged, taking the heavy bottle in my hands and leaning in for a long swig. It wasn't the most pleasant thing I'd ever put to my lips, but I swallowed it easily and passed it on. "Let the party start," I giggled.

My friend and I passed the bottle around the rest of the night until it was empty. My stomach now hurt, and the room began to spin around me

Stories from the Oasis

as I stumbled into bed. "I'm officially drunk," I laughed. My friend laughed, too, which made me feel good.

I liked being a part of the in crowd, sharing secrets and trying new things. With each new experiment, I increased my odds of staying popular.

When I turned 16, I got my driver's license. I could hardly wait to take my truck out for a spin. A license was a sure way to win the hearts of pretty girls in my class!

It also served as the perfect transportation to the nearest nightclubs, where I began partying with my peers.

In my eyes, I'd finally achieved just what I'd been reaching for all these years: true popularity.

During my senior year of high school, I found a new love: cocaine. The first time I snorted the harmless-seeming powder, I knew I'd struck gold. Pot and beer were fun, but this opened up a whole new world! I continued to snort it every chance I got, and by the end of the year, school and sports were taking a backseat to my new best friend — cocaine.

One evening, at a party, I got caught with cocaine and was arrested. I was devastated. I'd always been known as a decent fellow around our small town of Rockwall, and suddenly, my reputation

Outside Prison Walls

was tarnished. Drinking and partying was one thing, but getting arrested was plain mortifying!

When I returned to school, my baseball coach told me that if I was convicted of a felony, I would be kicked out of school. For a while, I was stressed out about the possibility of my arrest ruining my chances of graduating high school. Thankfully, the trial was postponed until after graduation. So I earned my diploma and one year of probation, as well.

I spent the next year trying to get clean. With the pressures of high school behind me, I no longer needed to uphold an image. I used this chance to clear my head and figure out what I was going to do with my life.

By the time my year of probation was up, I had found work and resumed partying. It started with a few beers, and before long, I was back to my old ways. I fell in love with cocaine, again, and realized how much I missed getting high. Coke gave me a lightning zap of energy that kept me on my toes all day. I continued to fool myself into thinking I could live a double life, keeping up with my work, while doing drugs on the sidelines.

I found a tech school in Waco, Texas, that sounded interesting and left the comforts of my small hometown for an adventure in the big city. I was determined to get my act together in college, but it was only a matter of weeks before I was back to my old ways. The beer, women and drugs flowed like never before. I dabbled with heroin, ecstasy and anything else I could get my hands on. College popularity, I soon learned, was even better than high school stuff. With money to support my habit, I could live it up like never before!

One evening, coming back from Padre Island after a weekend of partying, I heard dreaded sirens behind me on the highway. I'd downed a bottle of Vodka before I hit the road and had set the cruise control at 90 miles per hour. There was no doubt that I'd been speeding.

"Crap!" I muttered under my breath. Pulling the car to the side of the road, I smoothed my rumpled t-shirt, trying to look presentable. I had grown accustomed to charming people wherever I went.

Perhaps I can charm the cop, and he'll go on his merry way.

"You been drinking, son? You were going 90 in a 55." The cop frowned at me from the window.

My legs trembled as I shook my head. *Play it cool, Shane.* "Had a beer a few hours ago," I lied. I wondered if my words were slurred. Surely, this cop was no dummy.

Outside Prison Walls

"Please step out of the car, son," the cop replied, obviously not convinced of my story.

I took a deep breath and opened the car door. I knew the drill. Walk the line, put one foot in front of the other. *Concentrate, Shane! You can do this!*

Things didn't go my way that evening. The cop slapped me with a DWI, and before I knew it, I was back on probation for another year. I knew it was time to get my act together, once and for all. I couldn't go on this way, playing with fire. Next time, a cold cement jail cell could be waiting for me if I didn't stop messing around.

A year after quitting school, I returned home to Rockwall, ready to begin my future. I seriously contemplated starting my own landscaping business. From my rough deductions, the money would be good, and the work would be relatively easy. With a new goal in mind, I put my partying on the back burner and worked my way down to a couple beers, here and there.

A year later, my business was up and running. I had several employees working for me and every reason to believe I would be successful. I purchased my first house in the rural outskirts of Rockwall, a major accomplishment for a guy my age. I dabbled with pot again and resumed drinking in moderation but steered clear of heavy drugs.

Stories from the Oasis

Until one day, when my world spiraled and was turned upside down, once again.

"Hey, you ever tried this s***?" My buddy and I had just arrived at the bass pro shop when he shut the door and pulled out a small bag filled with white powder.

The rain pounded on the roof above, drowning out my thudding heart. I'd spent the last couple years nearly sober. *Would I really get lured into this stuff again?* "Whatcha got there?" I asked coolly, grabbing the bag from my friend.

"Meth, man. Crazy stuff. You ain't tried nothin' till you've tried this s***. You can literally stay up for days. It's insane." He grinned. "You wanna try?"

Suddenly, I was back in junior high again being handed my first joint. I shrugged and tried to play it cool. "Sure, why not?" I could use a little extra energy, I reasoned.

What's the harm?

It was love at first sniff. In a matter of moments, I was sucked into a world that would hold me in a death grip for the next few years. The following three days were spent doing as much meth as I could. Even as my gut screeched, "No!", I knew there was no turning back. I was hooked.

Being high on meth was a new low for me,

Outside Prison Walls

though I didn't see it at the time. Just as my friend had promised, it gave me the energy to stay awake for days, which meant kicking butt at my business. When I did finally lie down at night, it was because I had passed out, not because I'd fallen asleep. Slowly, my normally 185-pound frame shrunk to an emaciated 160 pounds.

Before long, I became a prisoner in my own home. The nights blurred into the days as I repeated the pattern of getting high and then crashing and burning. My world turned into a bizarre nightmare overnight. With several employees able to run the business for me, I spent more and more time away from the job site and locked in my bedroom. If I needed a fix, it was just a phone call away. Instead of dating, I hired prostitutes to come into my home. No need to head out into the social scene if everything I needed could come right to my doorstep. I convinced myself I was living the life, but inside I was trapped, dying, terrified.

"I need your help, Shane." My buddy called me one night. He'd found a way to get our hands on some copper pipes. We could sell them for a pretty penny to fellow meth users, who could, in turn, use them to churn out more drugs. "Meet me in front of your house in an hour. We need your truck."

"Oh, s***," I moaned, fumbling for something

Stories from the Oasis

to wear in my mounting pile of dirty clothes. My house looked like a tornado had ripped through it, but I hadn't the least bit of interest in picking up a broom. I shoved my feet into some shoes, splashed some water on my face and stumbled outside to wait for my buddy.

Darkness greeted us as we rumbled down the road in my truck a few minutes later, my heart thudding. "What if someone tries to kill us?" I threw out.

"No one's gonna kill us, man. You're so paranoid all the time. Stop actin' crazy. It's a simple heist. We cut the pipes, throw them in the back of your truck and split."

"All right." I stepped on the gas and wished my heart would stop racing. *How do I get talked into this stupid stuff?* My mind was a jumble of confusion as we sped down the dirt road toward our destination. Hopefully, the few hundred bucks we'd pocket would make this stupid trip worth it.

***

"I'm worried about you, Shane," my father said a few days later when he came to pay me a visit. "You never leave the house, and you look like death. Please, your mother and I are begging you

Outside Prison Walls

to get your life together. This is no way to live, son. You're going to lose everything." His pleading eyes showed genuine sadness.

I winked open an eye and rolled off the couch. "I'm fine, Dad, really," I muttered, throwing a t-shirt over my head. "Don't worry about me, all right?"

"But I *am* worried. You have us all worried. Your mother sends me over here just to make sure you're still breathing. You've missed the last three family dinners we've had. This isn't like you. Now, tell me what's going on and how I can get you help."

Let's see, Dad. I'm a meth junkie, and I haven't slept in three days. I spend $100 to $300 a day to support my drug habit. Is that what you want to hear?

I sighed and tried to appease my father with my words. "I'm fine, all right? Just trust me." Even as I uttered the words, I knew I was anything but fine. I was a prisoner in my own worst nightmare, and I hadn't a clue as to how to wake up.

My father's warning about losing everything couldn't have rung more true. Not only had I alienated myself from my friends and family, but my business was in jeopardy. Within weeks, I was forced to sell it. Everything I'd worked so hard for

Stories from the Oasis

had been lost to a drug that had taken over my life. I was devastated.

"I know why I'm in this mess," I told my mother one afternoon, standing across from her in her sunny kitchen. I rarely ventured out of my prison, but I needed a few bucks and hoped my parents might be able to spot me some cash.

"Why, son?" My mother's eyes were sad and weary, devoid of hope.

"My pride, Mom. My pride's gotten me where I'm at, and it's gonna take a miracle to get me out."

My mother sighed. "At least you can see that much, son," she said quietly. "Your father and I are praying for you."

Tears spilled down my cheeks as I headed home that evening. I knew the lifestyle I was engaged in was wrong. It grieved my parents, and deep down, I knew it grieved God. I had always believed in him; my childhood days spent in Sunday school often came to mind. I was too terrified to talk to God, though, after all I had done. Surely he didn't want anything to do with a messed up junkie like me.

A few weeks later, a sharp rap on the door jolted me out of my drug-induced sleep. I threw on some sweats and stumbled to the front door. "Yeah?" I muttered, cracking it open.

Outside Prison Walls

"Task force. We have a warrant to search your house."

I peered through the door and saw a man holding up a badge. My heart caught in my throat as I pulled back the door.

"What for?" I asked innocently.

"Possession of marijuana and meth," the officer replied, pushing open the door with force. His eyes fell onto the mounting pile of dirty clothes, dishes and crumpled beer cans strewn around the living room. He cleared his throat and stepped over the filth. "You've been growing pot," he said. It was not a question, but more of a statement.

I shrugged and tried to keep my cool. My buddies and I had been growing pot out back, but I was so far out in the country, I figured no one would ever notice. "Don't know what you're talkin' about," I replied nonchalantly, flopping back on the couch. My head spun, and my knees grew weak. I needed another fix, and now this guy had come and rudely interrupted everything! Irritated, I glared at him as he began rummaging through my drawers and cupboards. *Isn't this invasion of privacy?*

I was arrested and taken to jail, where I failed a drug test. Things weren't looking good for this hometown boy. With no legitimate way of making

Stories from the Oasis

money, I was on a fast track to nowhere.

While I was out on probation, my actions from a few months prior caught up with me in a real sort of way. It was 1:30 a.m., and I was startled, once again, to hear a loud rapping on the front door. Pulling myself out of bed, confused and disoriented, I stumbled to the front door and cracked it open. Five dark-clothed strangers pushed their way inside. Two men held loaded pistols against my face, while another hit me over the head with a Maglite. I reeled with pain and then tried to regain my strength and fight back, but my head throbbed so badly I could hardly see straight. I felt my heart rate escalate because I knew what was going to happen next. I had owed the drug dealers money for months, and they were finally getting tired of trying to collect.

"Hand over the money! Hand over the money now!"

"I don't have it, man."

Then it came hard and fast. They pummeled me to the ground and beat me senseless.

Heart thudding, it crossed my mind that they had come to kill me. Instead, they stormed out, leaving me badly bruised and bleeding.

Not long after they left, a friend of mine showed up out of nowhere.

Outside Prison Walls

The timing could not have been more impeccable. "Oh, man, what happened?" My friend helped me to my feet, then cleaned and bandaged my cuts. "You're in bad shape, man," he muttered as he wiped the excess blood trickling down my face.

I nodded. "Yeah. Thank God you showed up just now," I mumbled weakly. The abrupt attack had left me in a state of shock. Afraid I might lose consciousness, I lay back on the couch and closed my eyes, wincing in pain.

"You better be more careful," my friend advised, standing to leave. "You gotta watch who you mess with, man. Those guys could have killed you."

The next morning, my dad arrived at my house shocked to see the state I was in. "Son, you could have been killed!" my father declared, echoing my friend's haunting words. "You've got to take care of yourself."

Drowsy from the drugs and the pain, I nodded and took in his words. I cared about my family. They had raised me to be an upright, caring young man. I knew my decisions hurt them deeply.

I could not go on living like this, but I had no idea how to get out of the deep hole I'd dug for myself. I was an unhappy man near the end of his rope. Perhaps my father and friend were right. The next time, I might not be so lucky. I might be dead.

The next few weeks were a whirlwind of legal nightmares and failed drug tests. My parents hired the best lawyers in town, but my case was looking dismal. I had been caught red-handed in possession of drugs and with drugs in my system. It didn't get much worse than that.

I went to jail for 40 days and crashed on a bed for the first four. My body was exhausted from all the drugs, so I just slept and slept.

When I finally woke up, I was met with a stark and sober reality, one that I did not want to look at. My life was a mess, my body was screwed up. I hated being sober. It was like looking into a very unflattering mirror of regrets with no drug-induced distractions.

"We can get you into rehab in Overton, located in east Texas," my probation officer told me. "This is your last chance to get your act together."

"I'll go," I agreed. It was the best choice I had — the options were jail or rehab. The arrest had turned out to be a blessing in disguise. Perhaps I would have gone on living in a filthy house, snorting meth for the rest of my life had I not been caught. Only later on would I realize that God had been orchestrating it all, allowing me to reach rock bottom so that I'd have nowhere to look but up.

Outside Prison Walls

***

"You will stay as long as you need to," my counselor told me during one of our first meetings. "I trust Overton will be well worth your time. It was very generous of the state to pay your way here. These programs are quite expensive, if I may be blunt."

"Thank you for this chance," I replied sincerely. I truly wanted to make my time here count.

Over the next few weeks, the scriptures my mother had shared with me throughout my childhood came pouring into my mind. I lay on my bed, chewing on them one by one. Suddenly, I was 10 years old again, sitting in Sunday school listening to the teacher talk about God's love for his children. *Where did that little boy go?* In my quest for popularity, I began heading down a sad and dangerous road, which could very well have ended in death. The more I studied, the more I realized that thanks to God's amazing grace, I no longer had to live that life. With his help, my life could be restored!

With ample time to spend alone, I found myself talking to God for the first time in years. "I know I screwed up real bad, and I'm sorry," I told the Lord, wondering if he might still hear my

Stories from the Oasis

prayers after all I had done. "Please help me find my way again. I need your help. Please come into my life." I felt a hundred pounds lighter as I said this simple prayer. Was it really possible that he might help me spin a U-turn after going down the wrong road all these years?

Each morning at Overton began with a short time of praise and worship followed by meditation and reading out of the Bible. Though Overton was not advertised as a Biblically-based 12-step program, I was pleased that God was a part of our daily routine.

I joined an *Experiencing God* Bible study, which I found to be wonderfully insightful. For the first time, I was learning how to have a true relationship with God. I had always thought of him as the big man upstairs, someone who dished out slaps on the wrist when I messed up, rather than a merciful God who loved to give second chances. I had often tossed God on the back burner when girls, drugs and partying came along. Slowly, I came to understand that, just as the study title suggested, I could experience God in every aspect of my life. He could become my best friend, someone whom I could speak with at all times, someone who cared about my deepest hurts and my greatest joys.

Outside Prison Walls

"Thank you, Lord, for not giving up on me," I prayed one night as I headed back from the study. "All these years when I set you aside, you never forgot about me. Thank you for this second chance. I want to make my life right, once and for all."

My eyes fell onto James 1:2 as I flipped open my Bible that night. "Count it all joy when you experience trials." I had certainly experienced trials, but thanks to God's amazing grace, I could learn to find forgiveness, peace and even joy despite my circumstances. Once again, I praised the Lord for intervening in my life, bringing me to Overton and to my knees.

"How come you're always readin' your Bible?" one of my peers asked me one day after lunch. "You're always prayin' and whistlin' hymns under your breath and stuff. How come?"

"I've finally found a true relationship with God," I explained. Since entering the rehab facility, I had learned to grow bold in my renewed faith. Most of the 70 residents, it seemed, wanted little to do with God. Questions like this gave me ample opportunity to describe the journey God had taken me on, ending with finding true peace in him. "If you want to know more, I'd love to talk to you," I added hopefully.

Stories from the Oasis

He shrugged. "Yeah, maybe. Cool."

The days grew into weeks, and I found myself quite lonely at times. There was no doubt I needed to stay in the facility to get well, but at times, I grew antsy for companionship. One evening, on my way to dinner, I met a pretty girl in the hall. I had seen her a time or two, but our shoulders hadn't so much as touched as we passed. This time, however, I made an effort to say hello.

She smiled and introduced herself. We spent the next few days talking, comparing stories and sharing a few laughs. I could not deny my strong physical attraction to her. One night, when all the lights had gone out, I snuck over to her room. We engaged in physical relations, which was against policy in the rehab center. The moment I left her room, a wave of guilt ran through my veins. I knew I had not only let God down but myself and the facility, as well. The fact that we hadn't been caught did little to appease my guilt. It ate at me for days.

One night, as I returned to my room after Bible study, I found myself tossing and turning for hours. I could think of nothing but the inappropriate act with the girl. A battle waged in my mind. If I confessed my indiscretion, I would be kicked out of the program and perhaps even arrested. I had

Outside Prison Walls

been doing so well at Overton, whizzing through the steps with flying colors. It would be a shame to end it all now.

"You need to confess, Shane." It was as if God himself was standing in front of me speaking these words. There was no use ignoring them. I heard him loud and clear. "Confess what you've done."

Trembling, I gulped and yanked the covers over my head. "But, God, what if this is the end for me?" I cried out. Tears filled my eyes at the thought of being arrested and kicked out of the program. How would I ever get back on my feet after that?

"Be still, and know that I am God." Again, the words came out of nowhere but were unmistakably clear. God had a powerful message for me, one I could not ignore. I shot up in bed as the tears spilled down my cheeks. I knew, without a doubt, what had to be done.

The next morning, I rushed to call my accountability partner from my Bible study. "I did something bad in the rehab center," I told him sheepishly and proceeded to confess my actions.

"You need to come clean, Shane. It's not the easy thing to do, but it's the right thing to do."

That night, I tossed and turned in my bed, my friend's words heavy upon my heart. "God, I don't

Stories from the Oasis

know if I can do this," I cried out as I yearned for sleep that night. The idea of coming clean to my supervisors, who had seen me make amazing strides in the program, was devastating. How could I let them down?

"Be still, and know that I am God." Again, there were those words comforting me like a warm blanket. God did not say, "Be still, and know everything is going to be fine." Instead, he merely asked me to trust in him.

As sleep called to me that night, I embraced it and knew, somehow, that everything was going to be all right.

The next morning, with trembling hands and a pounding heart, I confessed my inappropriate act. Just as I had predicted, the counselors implored that I would most likely be arrested and sent back to jail. "This was your last chance, Shane, and I'm afraid you haven't complied with our rules," was their firm response.

Sure enough, the next day I was taken to the local jail. My parents were notified right away. I was terribly saddened that I had let them down as they had worked so hard to get me into the rehab facility. Nevertheless, I was filled with an unexplainable peace, unlike anything I'd ever known.

The moment the cell doors slammed shut, I hit

Outside Prison Walls

my knees and began to sob. Dozens of other men sat around on the bunks, staring at me as I wept. Little did they know that I was weeping because I had never felt so close to God in my entire life. I had done what he'd asked me to do, and things didn't look promising for me. But even through it all, I felt his grace shine through. He had not given up on me, nor had he forsaken me in my darkest hour. Though the walls closed in on me in the tiny cement cell, I felt freer than I had in years.

Once I got to jail, I called my father.

"How are you holding up, son?"

"It's okay, Dad," I assured him softly. "I feel better than I have in my entire life. I've honestly never felt more like a man."

"You're kidding, right?" my dad replied, raising his brow.

I shook my head. "Nope. I'm dead serious. I feel this total peace, like God is right here with me, helping me to hang on. I'm not afraid of the future. I'll take what comes my way. I know now that he will never leave me."

My dad gave a low whistle. "I admire you, son, and I'm happy to see you growing. Your mother and I are both praying, as well as many other people at church. Let's pray we can get you out of there soon."

Stories from the Oasis

"Thanks, Dad," I whispered.

That Monday, I was transferred back to the Rockwall County Prison, and Pastor Barney from Oasis Church came to pay me a visit. His warm eyes and genuine smile suggested I could be completely open with him. "You look good," he said, grinning as I sat down across from him.

I laughed. "My dad said orange isn't my color."

"Well, okay, maybe not your best color. Anyhow, how are you holding up, Shane? You doing all right?"

"I'm doing great," I replied sincerely. "I've had lots of time to talk with God, and I genuinely feel like he is going to take care of me. I don't know what's going to happen, but it's okay because it's all in his hands."

"That's wonderful." Pastor Barney beamed. "Would you mind if I prayed with you before I left, son?"

"That would be great," I replied. It was a wonderful feeling to know hundreds of people were rallying behind me in prayer. I was not ashamed that they knew of my troubles. I wanted to come clean before the world so that God could receive all the glory through my struggles.

That night, as I headed to bed, I prayed I might get a good night's sleep. Living with two dozen

Outside Prison Walls

men in a jail cell could grow quite tense. I climbed into bed and pulled the thin cover over my head. The TV droned in the background, nearly drowned out by the arguing of two men nearby. *Please, Lord, help me. I don't want to be here.*

For a moment, I felt like Peter walking toward Jesus on the water. I believed, but for a second, my faith wavered, and I felt myself slowly sinking. What if my parents' attorney couldn't help me out? I'd be sentenced to months or even years in a rehab prison! Once again, I felt God's simple words warm my soul. *Be still, and know that I am God.*

"Okay, Lord," I prayed, "I believe you. No matter what the outcome of my situation, I will trust in you."

Thanksgiving came and went. Instead of enjoying turkey and gravy with my family, I dined on a bland, cold meal with my cellmates. Loneliness overcame me for a moment as I thought of my loved ones back home. How I yearned to be sitting at that table, sharing laughter with them. Never again would I miss a family function because of my selfish ways!

The following Monday, my counselor called with wonderful news. "The court overrode the recommendation for rehab prison," she told me. "You're going to be a free man!"

Stories from the Oasis

"Praise God!" I shouted, aware that several other hard-looking men were peering over my shoulder. If God wanted to use me in this prison, so be it. I would not be ashamed of my faith. My God had delivered me like Daniel in the lion's den. Praise belongs to him!

The moment I got out of jail, I threw myself back into church. It was wonderful to set foot in the place I had spent my childhood years worshipping. The congregation of Oasis Church embraced me like the prodigal son, welcoming me with open arms and kind words of encouragement. I realized, at once, that I not only had my immediate family but an entire church family to lean on, as well. I would never again be alone.

A few months after I began my new life, I ran into an old buddy whom I used to use drugs with. His eyes were bloodshot, his clothes rumpled and his skin pale and scabbed. I had to keep myself from gasping as I saw what very well could have been my own reflection, years ago. "How are you doing?" I asked sincerely. "It's good to see you, man."

"You, too," he slurred, grabbing my hand. "Good to see you."

As I walked away that afternoon, I couldn't get the image of my old friend out of my mind. *That*

Outside Prison Walls

was me. Thankfully, I was now addicted to Jesus! I made it a goal to pray each night that this young man would find his way.

Having come so far since my drug days, I saw it only fitting to give back to a community who had so graciously bestowed their love and prayers upon me. I enrolled in a school of ministry, knowing only that I wanted to share with the world the good news of my gracious heavenly father, who did not give up on me, even during my darkest hour. He is faithful, merciful and loving, and I want others to know him as I do.

My relationship with my family has been restored. Today, we are closer than ever. No longer do I take for granted family dinners and other special occasions. I have truly been blessed with a wonderful family who not only love me despite my imperfections but loves the great God we serve, as well.

My life is not perfect now, but I look at things a little differently.

When challenges come along, instead of using drugs to deal with my circumstances, I remember the verse that saved my life during those long days at Overton:

"Consider it pure joy, my brothers, whenever you face trials of many kinds, because you know

Stories from the Oasis

that the testing of your faith develops perseverance. Perseverance must finish its work so that you may be mature and complete, not lacking anything." (James 1:2)

Now I accept those challenges head-on with God, my Savior, by my side.

Conclusion

These are just some of the testimonies of lives that have been gloriously changed and transformed by making right decisions and trusting in an almighty God. These people are neither idols nor icons. They live among us; they are a part of our community. We at Oasis Church commend each person whose life experiences are found on these pages and testify to their authenticity.

Jesus said, "Come to me, all you who labor and are heavy laden, and I will give you rest. Take my yoke upon you and learn from me, for I am gentle and lowly in heart, and you will find rest for your souls." (Matthew 11:28-29, NKJV)

Accept the fact that Jesus loves you, and you need a Savior. "For the wages of sin is death, but the gift of God is eternal life in Christ Jesus our Lord." (Romans 6:23, NIV)

Believe that God, your Father, wishes to fill your new heart with his life. "I will give them singleness of heart and put a new spirit within them. I will take away their hearts of stone and give them tender hearts instead ..." (Ezekiel 11:19, NLT)

"What this means is that those who become Christians become new persons. They are not the

Stories from the Oasis

same anymore, for the old life is gone. A new life has begun!" (2 Corinthians 5:17, NLT)

Believe that God, your Father, can transform your whole life through Jesus Christ. "…take on an entirely new way of life — a God-fashioned life, a life renewed from the inside and working itself into your conduct as God accurately reproduces his character in you." (Ephesians 4:22-24, The MESSAGE)

Confess your sins to Jesus and receive from him eternal life. "If we confess our sins, he is faithful and just and will forgive us our sins and purify us from all unrighteousness." (1 John 1:9, NIV)

Pray: Lord Jesus, I recognize that my sin is killing me physically, emotionally and spiritually. I need you to give me a new heart so your life can come and fill me. I recognize I am a sinner and need to be forgiven so I can escape your judgment. I believe your blood has forgiven my sins, and I receive your forgiveness. I welcome your holiness into my new heart. I give myself to you so you can begin to remake and transform me. Amen.

Now, share what has happened to you with another believer! Find a church family that can help you receive complete healing, and discover God's plan and purpose in the earth.

We would love for you to join us!

We meet Sunday mornings at 10 a.m. at 5026 Locust Grove, Garland, TX 75043.

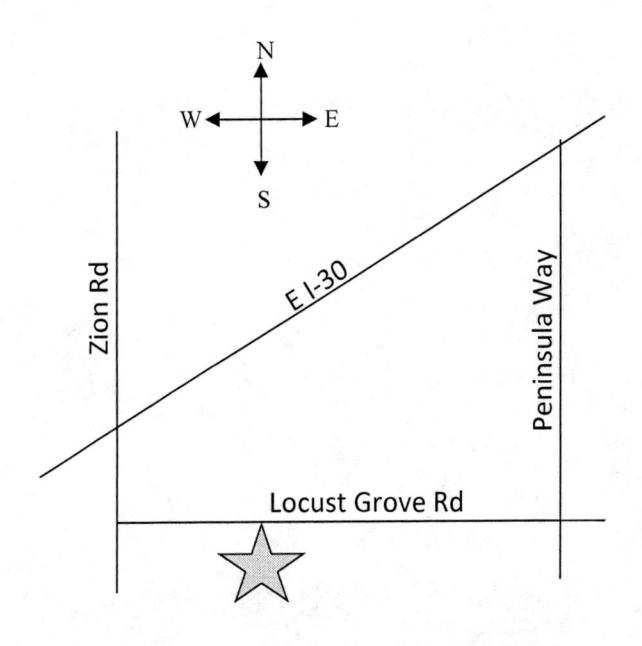

Please call us at 972.203.3522 for directions, or contact us at www.ioasis.org.

For more information on reaching your city with stories from your church, please contact Good Catch Publishing at www.goodcatchpublishing.com

Good Catch Publishing

Did one of these stories touch you?
Did one of these real people move you to tears?
Tell us (and them) about it on our reader blog at
www.goodcatchpublishing.blogspot.com.